COMPARATIVE POLITICAL VIOLENCE

PRENTICE-HALL
CONTEMPORARY COMPARATIVE POLITICS SERIES
JOSEPH LaPALOMBARA, Editor

FRED R. VON DER MEHDEN

Rice University

Prentice-Hall, Inc.,
Englewood Cliffs, N.J.

COMPARATIVE
POLITICAL
VIOLENCE

Library of Congress Cataloging in Publication Data

von der Mehden, Fred R.
  Comparative political violence.

  Bibliography: p.
  1. Violence. 2. World politics—1945–
I. Title. II. Title: Political violence.
JC328.6.V6   301.5′92   72-5761
ISBN 0–13–153999–X
ISBN 0–13–153981–7 (pbk.)

COMPARATIVE POLITICAL VIOLENCE
Fred R. von der Mehden

Printed in the United States of America

10   9   8   7   6   5   4   3   2   1

PRENTICE-HALL INTERNATIONAL, INC., London
PRENTICE-HALL OF AUSTRALIA, PTY. LTD., Sydney
PRENTICE-HALL OF CANADA, LTD., Toronto
PRENTICE-HALL OF INDIA PRIVATE LIMITED, New Delhi
PRENTICE-HALL OF JAPAN, INC., Tokyo

to my brother Roy

CONTENTS

FOREWORD

This volume on political corruption is the first in a series on Contemporary Comparative Politics that has been several years in the planning stage. The organization of the series is based on a number of assumptions and guidelines that are worth calling to the reader's attention. Foremost among these is that the undergraduate student of comparative politics is less interested in political science than we might hope, but more capable of synthetic analysis than we may imagine. If this is so, then it would be an enormous mistake to pretend to organize an introductory series around one or more half-baked "theories" of politics or political systems—theories that are difficult for even the more hardened members of the profession to digest. It would seem equally debatable whether the undergraduate student has a strong desire to learn in depth the institutional arrangements and workings of any single political system, whether that system be as established as that of Great Britain or as new and exotic as that of Tanzania.

What, then, can we expect of those undergraduates who study comparative politics? First, I think that they are quickly turned off by simplistic or spurious efforts to lend the discipline a theoretical elegance it manifestly does not possess; second, that saturation treatments of single political systems are as unpalatable today when the countries are individually packaged as they were when several countries appeared between the same hard covers; and third, that the undergraduates sitting in our classrooms might very well be turned on if they learned what sorts of things political scientists do and what kinds of knowledge of the political process they can glean from the things we do. These things, incidentally, would involve not merely data-gathering on some aspect of the political system, but also speculative and normative considerations about the relationship between politics and the good life. We can expect that if the things to be written and lectured about are carefully chosen and intelligently organized, the undergraduate will display a striking capacity to synthesize information and to develop skills in analyzing political phenomena at least as impressive as, say, those of a New York taxi driver, a voluble parent, or a political orator.

Another major assumption underlying the organization of the series is that the topics included should not reflect a commitment to an institutional or behavioral, normative or empirical approach. If members of the profession are still battling about such things, let them spare undergraduates the arid, scholastic, and essentially unproductive nature of such encounters. The authors of this series are neither bare-facts empiricists nor "cloud-ninety" political moralists; they neither sanctify nor abominate institutional or behavioral analysis but would rather use whatever methods are available to enlighten the reader about important aspects of political life. To emphasize the important is also to be relevant, and our correlative assumption here is that the student who wants political science to be "relevant" does not mean by this that it should be banal, simple-minded, or unsystematic.

Since no series can tell us everything about politics, we have had to choose what we consider to be the important, relevant, and reasonably integrated topics. Such choices are always arbitrary to some extent. However, we have sought to accord attention to certain standard and ubiquitous institutions as well as to newer conceptual and analytical foci that have provoked a good deal of recent research and discussion. Thus, the series will have a volume on Comparative Legal Cultures, but another on Comparative Political Violence; it will include a fine volume on Constitutionalism, and one on Revolutionary Movements.

Volumes to follow this one will represent what we believe is an interesting and useful mosaic that should be appealing to those who teach, those who learn about, and all of those who try to understand politics.

JOSEPH LAPALOMBARA

New Haven

PREFACE

This study grows out of a long acquaintance with political violence in Southeast Asia and a fear that Americans have not viewed their own internal conflict with sufficient international and ideological persp⌐ctive. This is an attempt to expand our cognition of the types, justifications, and causes of political violence throughout the world during the post-war years.

This book was made possible through the generous support of the Center for Research in Social Change and Economic Development and Program of Development Studies of Rice University. I also wish to thank Professors John Ambler, Robert Dix, George Antunes and Robert Pendley of the Department of Political Science of Rice University for advice and comment on specific sections of the manuscript. Mr. Kim Q. Hill compiled the aggregate data tables for the final chaper and that part would never have been completed without his meticulous and often difficult search for data. Finally, my thanks to Miss Jaquie Ehlers who worked through the summer heat of Houston typing the final manuscript. Of course, if any violence was done to the comments and data of those who have helped me in this enterprise, I am the single causal factor.

F. VON DER MEHDEN

COMPARATIVE POLITICAL VIOLENCE

TYPES AND JUSTIFICATION OF POLITICAL VIOLENCE

part one

INTRODUCTION

1

Violence has become an "in" subject for scholar and politician alike in the United States. The assassinations of the Kennedys and Rev. Martin Luther King, Jr., when combined with ghetto riots and campus demonstrations, have led to serious reflection on the role of domestic political conflict. However, if the American citizen is in danger of being overwrought by the picture of his country as a uniquely "sick" or "violent" society, he might consider, for example, that during the last half of the 1960s Black Africa, with a population similar in size to that of the United States, experienced violent coup attempts in a majority of its states, tribal or religious conflict in more than twenty states, student violence resulting in death or injury in over a dozen countries, one bloody civil war, and the execution for treason of military and civilian leaders in every part of the continent. Rather than simply decrying political violence, therefore, we must seek understanding of it through careful analysis of the types of domestic strife that have confronted the world in the postwar era.

The variety of violent events is so great and the problems of explanation are so complex that it is necessary to define carefully the exact scope of this book. The study that follows is not intended to cover all aspects of domestic violence, nor will it investigate international conflict. Nor is it intended to duplicate previously developed analyses of data.[1] This book will instead attempt to describe various types and justifications for political violence and to view in depth some of the more salient explanations for its appearance. The Introduction seeks both to set forth some of the problems attendant to the study of violence and to analyze some of the types of domestic conflict experienced in the postwar era. Chapter 2 describes the

[1] See, for example, Gurr, 1970; Graham and Gurr, 1969; Nieburg, 1969; Pye, 1956; Eckstein, 1963: Huntington, 1968.

bases upon which individuals and groups justify the necessity to employ violence to achieve political goals. These include primordial, ideological, and specific issue-oriented legitimizations. The third chapter moves into the area of "establishment violence," an issue often clouded by polemics. The various types of violence used by the state against opponents, and the state's rationale for such practices, are examined in detail. The chapters grouped in Part II engage three of the major causes of political conflict put forward by scholars and politicians—economic and social deprivation, the communal-class conflict syndrome, and a lack of societal legitimacy.

Each of these last chapters is an effort to employ different methodologies, primarily the comparative case method and the use of aggregate data. It is recommended that those unfamiliar with specific foreign examples of mass political violence first view Chapters 4 and 5 to acquaint themselves with the rudimentary facts.

ASSESSING POLITICAL VIOLENCE

Any comparative analysis of political violence must wrestle with the conceptual problems of defining what is meant by the terms "violence" and "political" in this context. In general, the concept of violence includes acts such as killing, injuring, raping, or forcibly stealing from others. When we attempt to establish the political orientation of such violence or to judge the relative influence of such acts upon the political system, however, this simple definition of violence becomes clouded as problems of definition and data become highly complex. At a time when strikes and demonstrations take place over a wide variety of issues or when various "radical" groups describe the very existence of certain institutions as acts of political violence, the problems of definition become particularly acute. For example, is a land reform riot a political or an economic act? Is the violence involved in an anti-clerical struggle to be described as religious or profane? To what extent is an assassination of a local leader in a remote village due to political or to personal animosities?

Difficulties over the reliability of data on political violence are significant and make any type of aggregate analysis suspect. In many countries police reports are inadequate, newspapers are controlled in what they can report, contact with rural areas is infrequent, and objective outside investigators may be unavailable. Reports of increased violence simply may be a result of better systems of crime statistics, just as, conversely, reports of decreased violence may be based upon the political decision of a ministry of information as to what is to be reported. Examples of wide disparities in reporting are multitudinous. The number of Communists executed in Indonesia in 1965–66 has variously been reported between 80,000 and a million while government censorship or an absence of foreign reporters made it impossible to obtain trustworthy reports of the 1971 civil war in Pakistan, the executions of Tibetans by Chinese after the Communist victory in Tibet, the killing of Indians in Brazil, and deaths of Vietnamese in Cambodia in 1970. The reliability of violence data becomes particularly suspect when ideological issues are involved. Events such as the Hungarian uprising, Indonesian anti-Communist activities, the assassination of village leaders in Vietnam, and trials of landowners in post-1949 mainland China are clouded by conflicting statements by partisans. In some cases there even may be denials that violence was present.

Finally, we must assess the difficulty of weighting the relative impact of different types of violent acts on varied political systems. Is a moderate degree of conflict over a long period to be given greater or lesser weight than a short-lived period of intense violence? In a country where political violence is normally high, would a given act of violence be weighed more or less heavily than the occurrence of the same act in a normally quiescent state? For example, an assassination in northeast Thailand or Vietnam may go unnoticed whereas the impact of such an event in Sweden or Switzerland would be considerable. In some countries violence may become an accepted act in the political sphere—a case, as it were, of what Hannah Arendt has called "the banality of evil." It is this consideration, among other factors, that makes it difficult to compare or to judge on a cross-national basis. Thus, levels of violence in terms of numbers of injuries and deaths, extent of property destruction, frequency of demonstrations, and so forth, may not provide very precise guidelines as to the relative impact of that level of violence on a particular body politic at a particular time.

The present analysis of political violence uses a limited definition in an effort to obviate some of the difficulties in evaluation. Violence will be discussed only as a group phenomenon. Individual acts of assassination, for example, will not be considered unless they are part of a wider program. Thus, unless further evidence is developed, the assassinations of the two Kennedys will not be brought into this analysis whereas the deaths of Patrice Lumumba or of the generals in the abortive 1965 Indonesian coup will be discussed because they were part of larger efforts. Secondly, an act will be treated here as an act of *political* violence if and only if it is an incident or part of a series of incidents intended by its perpetrators to influence local or national political decisions. In addition, acts of group violence will be brought into consideration if they influence those making national policy whether or not this was part of the intent of the group. Thus communal riots may be interpersonal in motivation but may strongly affect government and therefore fall into the scope of this study. For obvious reasons, international war will not be discussed. The following definition, by H. L. Nieburg, appears to cover much of what is considered herein:

acts of disruption, destruction, injury whose purpose, choice of targets or victims, surrounding circumstances, implementation, and/or effects have political significance, that is, tend to modify the behavior of others in a bargaining situation, that has consequences for the social system.[2]

TYPOLOGIES OF POLITICAL VIOLENCE

Political violence as considered in this volume is of five basic types: (1) Primordial (such as religious and racial); (2) Separatist or secessionist; (3) Revolutionary and counter-revolutionary; (4) Coup-oriented; (5) Political issues- and/or personality-oriented.

These categories are not to be considered either necessarily causal in nature or totally comprehensive. They are intended to include the vast majority of acts of political violence and are presented to provide a more systematic evaluation of the types of political violence that have been experienced in the postwar era. We shall say something briefly about each category.

PRIMORDIAL VIOLENCE

This rubric covers acts of violence related to cultural—primarily racial or ethnic and religious—conflict. Often it is difficult to separate out the political element in these events from personal or group antagonisms. Although the individual employing this type of violence may not be attempting to influence political decision-making, the ultimate impact can be highly political in nature. In the twentieth century this kind of conflict has led to the largest number of deaths outside of international war. In the period prior to 1945 the Turkish actions against Greeks and Armenians and the Nazi liquidation of Jews come quickly to mind, while the postwar era has experienced mass slaughter of Hindus in Pakistan and Moslems in India, civil wars in Nigeria, the Sudan, and Rwanda, and violent outbreaks with religious or racial dimensions in Indonesia, Burma, Cambodia, and Zanzibar among others. Countries where postwar or post-independence violent events were primarily related to primordial factors are listed in Table 1–1. (Note that one country can be included on more than one list if there is a multiplicity of violent events.)

There is considerable variation in the events grouped together in this listing. Only Northern Ireland of the European (broadly defined) countries showed large-scale deaths (one hundred or more). It was also the only conflict that has been primarily religious in nature. The Italian and Spanish

[2] Nieburg, 1969, p. 13.

Table 1-1   Postwar or Post-Independence Primordial Violence

Africa	Asia	Europe *	Latin America	Middle East & North Africa
Congo (B)	Cambodia	United Kingdom	Brazil	Iran
Congo (K)	Laos	Italy	Guyana	Israel
Nigeria	Thailand	Spain		Sudan
Rwanda	Burma	Belgium		Lebanon
Burundi	Singapore	United States		Iraq
Tanzania	Malaysia	Canada		Egypt
Kenya	Indonesia			Afghanistan
Ethiopia	India			Turkey
Uganda	China (C)			Yemen
S. Africa	Ceylon			
Zambia	Philippines			
Dahomey	Vietnam			
Ghana	China (T)			
Chad	Pakistan			
Liberia				
Ivory Coast				
Equitorial Guinea				
Gabon				
Malagasy				
Niger				
Somalia				
Mauritania				

* Includes the U.S., Canada, Australia, and New Zealand. The following charts reflect all events for which there was sufficient information to justify inclusion within the particular category.

cases involved small minority groups, the Belgian instance centered on a low-level linguistic-cultural rivalry, and the Canadian instance was part of a complex problem related to its French Catholic population. Only the United States displayed an extended period of moderate-level (3–99 deaths per event) conflict related to race.[3]

Racially and religiously oriented conflict has been considerably more bloody in Afro-Asia than in Europe or the Western hemisphere in the postwar era. Perhaps half a million people died in the Moslem-Hindu massacres that followed partition of India and Pakistan in 1947. In Burma large-scale deaths and injuries took place in the civil war between the Burmese and Karens, Chins, Kachins, Mons and Arakanese. Extensive violence was to be found in Indonesia in a variety of conflicts involving Christian separatists against the Moslem majority, the Moslem zealot Dar-ul

[3] Low level   = 1–2 deaths or injuries per event
   Moderate level = 3–99 deaths or injuries per event
   High level   = 100 or more deaths or injuries per event

Islam movement against co-religionists, and Sumatran ethnic groups against the allegedly Javanese-dominated central government. Ceylon had its ethnic and religious divisions; the Chinese Communists reportedly carried out near genocide against the Tibetans and particularly against the Buddhist theocracy; Vietnamese killed indigenous Cambodians and vice versa; and the Kurds were targets of government attacks in the Middle East. Indeed, small-scale cases of domestic political violence with religious or ethnic connotations were reported in every country in East, Southeast, and South Asia. If one includes the domestic attacks against Jews in Arab countries related to the Arab-Israeli conflict, then almost all of the Middle East has also been subject to similar violence.

When most African states received their independence in the middle of the postwar era it was predicted that the artificial boundaries established by European colonial governments yoked together mutually antagonistic groups that would soon take up arms, one against the other. Recent history has given evidence to support this view as the vast majority of new states have experienced tribal or religiously oriented political violence.

Conflicts involving large-scale deaths and injuries have taken place between primordial groups in Rwanda, Burundi, the Congo (Kinshasa), Sudan, Zanzibar, Nigeria, and Uganda, while lower-level conflict has broken out elsewhere. Information on these events is often poorly reported or unreported. In the massacre of 10,000 or more Tutsi in Rwanda in the 1960s one reporter commented, "Not a single African state except Burundi raised a voice in protest. Not a word came from any other nation, western or eastern." [4]

SEPARATIST OR SECESSIONIST VIOLENCE

Separatist conflict is a particular form of primordial violence related to efforts by groups to achieve independence, autonomy, or special communal rights from the central government. (See Table 1–2.) Such events usually are tied to religious and ethnic divisions. They differ from the events associated with what we have called primordial violence, however, in that they are aimed at removing the aggrieved group from the sphere of influence of the group that dominates the central government. We reserve the term primordial violence for situations in which a group attempts to improve its situation by changing or altering conditions or even taking control of the central government, whereas the term secessionist violence

[4] Quoted in Lemarchand, 1970, p. 227. For a good analysis of the lack of general interest in the 1965 Indonesian massacres, see Brackman, 1969, pp. 120–26.

Table 1–2   Postwar or Post-Independence Separatist Violence

Africa	Asia	Europe	Latin America	Middle East & North Africa
Burundi	Philippines	Italy	Colombia *	Sudan
Nigeria	Burma	Spain		Iran
Congo (K)	Malaysia	Canada		Yemen
Ethiopia	Thailand	Belgium		Iraq
Rwanda	India			
Uganda	Pakistan			
Kenya	Indonesia			
Ivory Coast	China (C)			
Mauritania	China (T)			

* Colombia has experienced considerable regional violence. The extent of separatism in the conflict is open to question.

refers to situations in which a primordial fission runs so deep that efforts are directed at seceding from the sociopolitical context rather than at altering it. This situation is often associated with very high levels of political violence, as in the case of Ibo separatism in Nigeria, Chin, Kachin Shan, and Karen attacks on the Rangoon government in Burma, the formation of Bangladesh, the north-south, Moslem-Christian, Arab-Black dispute in the Sudan, and early efforts to dismember the former Belgian Congo. On the other hand, separatist efforts in Europe and North America have resulted in a comparatively low level of violence. Few or no deaths have been experienced in connection with French Canadian, Tyrolean, Basque, or Flemish demands, while this type of conflict has been almost totally absent from postwar Latin America. Only in Northern Ireland have separatist demands led to high levels of violence and even there other issues have probably been of equal consequence in escalating the conflict.

REVOLUTIONARY AND COUNTER-REVOLUTIONARY VIOLENCE

This is a limited classification that considers only political violence which takes place during the effort to overthrow a regime and to establish a state molded upon a significantly different economic/political model. Violence may be related to the actual revolutionary attack (Castro's overthrow of Batista or the Communist/Kuomintang Civil War of 1945–49), to counter-revolutionary reaction after a successful overthrow (the "Bay of Pigs" operation or the Hungarian uprising of 1956), or to postrevolutionary attempts to "fulfill" the revolution by cleansing the state of real or potential enemies (the trials in Cuba and China after the successes of the revolutionary forces). Regardless of whether or not it is successful, revolutionary violence of this sort may go on for quite some time, as is evidenced by the generation-long conflicts in Burma and Vietnam. These events must be carefully differentiated from coups which do not seek to fundamentally change the system, separatist movements, and anti-colonial wars. Thus, the 1958 military takeover in Burma would not be included in this category whereas the 1962 coup would be because it sought significant economic and political changes. Admittedly, this type of categorization must be somewhat arbitrary. In applying this classification we must be cautious about taking the statement of the proponents at face value. The fact that groups describe themselves as revolutionary does not tell us how apt the description might be.

Several observations pertain to the list in Table 1–3. Most violent efforts to establish revolutionary regimes were not successful, with only 20 percent of the struggles bringing the "revolution" to fruition. Of interest is the fact that among successful revolutionary states the greatest violence normally occurred in cases where the objective situation in which the revolution took place involved the aftermath of colonial administration or international conflict. In the postwar period, China, Burma, Cuba, and Bolivia have established successful revolutionary governments after winning their independence. (There is some question as to whether Sudan, Rwanda, Tanzania, Yemen, and Libya are to be included in this group.) A considerable number of the systems listed as revolutionary regimes—that is, regimes significantly different from their predecessors—were not established in the aftermath of independence, but arose out of colonial wars or military

Table 1–3 Postwar or Post-Independence Revolutionary and Counter-Revolutionary Violence

Africa	Asia	Europe	Latin America	Middle East & North Africa
Congo (K)	China (C)	Hungary	Cuba	Iran
Rwanda *	Cambodia	East Germany	Bolivia	Iraq
Tanzania *	Laos	Greece	Uruguay	Syria
	Thailand	Czechoslovakia	Colombia	Jordan
	N. & S. Vietnam		Venezuela	Yemen *
	Malaysia		Dominican Republic	Libya *
	Indonesia		Haiti	Turkey
	Burma		Guatemala *	Algeria
	Ceylon			Sudan *
	Korea			
	Philippines			
	Singapore			

There is some question as to whether the "revolutionary" party was the anti-government forces or the government.

occupation. (The east European states changed from authoritarian or democratic to Communist, West Germany and Japan from totalitarian and authoritarian to Western democratic, and Korea, Vietnam, and Algeria developed from colonial occupation.) In the European and Japanese cases revolutionary changes were largely nonviolent but they followed extremely bloody international conflicts.

Of the first four recognized revolutionary states mentioned above, Cuba displayed relatively low but significant levels of violence during all three periods (600 officially executed in the first five months after Castro's victory); Burma experienced only one accidental death in the coup of 1962, but the event followed fifteen years of sanguinary civil war and five years of heavy fighting across Burma in World War II; Bolivia was the scene of long periods of violence throughout its independent life; while China had the highest level of violence of all. Among the "questionable" revolutionary states only Libya experienced a comparatively peaceful history, as Tanzania (Zanzibar), Yemen, Rwanda, and Sudan all have gone through high-casualty civil wars that have left bitter memories and long-term antagonisms.

Of the unsuccessful revolutionary attempts, almost 75 percent have been led by Communist-oriented groups, with the remaining 25 percent primarily of an anti-Communist, counter-revolutionary nature. A significant number of the Communist-oriented revolutionary struggles have lasted over extended periods, with almost all of the Asian cases developing over the course of many years.

COUP-ORIENTED VIOLENCE

Successful or unsuccessful coups have been regular occurrences in the developing world but have not been much in evidence elsewhere. Within this category is considered violence attendant to efforts by organized groups to overthrow the regime in power without intending to establish fundamentally different economic/political systems. Again, decisions to apply this rubric are necessarily arbitrary, particularly when they involve assessing the intent of groups that fail to take power. The major successful perpetrators of coups are military personnel, whereas the failures tend to be the work of combinations of segments of the military and disgruntled politicians. In many African states it is often difficult to ascertain when one hears of an unsuccessful coup whether in fact a coup really had been planned, for there have been obvious cases where leaders have used trumped up charges to eliminate opponents.

It is interesting to note that most coups and coup attempts result in comparatively low levels of violence as either the military moves quickly

Table 1–4   Postwar or Post-Independence Coups and Attempted Coups
in which Violence Took Place

Africa	Asia	Europe	Latin America	Middle East & North Africa
Burundi	Indonesia	Greece	Colombia	Sudan
Chad	Thailand	Portugal	Bolivia	Egypt
Congo (K)	S. Korea		Argentina	Algeria
Congo (B)	Laos		Costa Rica	Syria
Cameroon	S. Vietnam		Cuba	Yemen
Sierra Leone	Cambodia		Dominican Republic	Turkey
Togo	Burma		Guatemala	Iraq
Somalia	Nepal		Haiti	Iran
Ghana			Nicaragua	Jordan
Malagasy			Panama	Libya
Malawi			Paraguay	Morocco
Zambia			Venezuela	Lebanon
Nigeria				
Equitorial Guinea				
Central African Rep.				
Upper Volta				
Rwanda				
Uganda				
Tanzania				
Gabon				
Niger				
Dahomey				
Ethiopia				
Guinea				
Ivory Coast				

to take power or the effort is "nipped in the bud." Usually only a few are killed and in the case of many attempts the largest number of deaths follows the coup as the losers are tried and executed for various offenses. For example, during one five-year period in the late 1960s, death sentences were passed against unsuccessful alleged coup leaders in the majority of new African states—a contrast to the situation in older Latin American and Southeast Asian countries, where the loser has normally found himself only jailed or exiled.

Table 1–4 lists countries experiencing coups and attempted coups in the postwar period.

POLITICAL ISSUE- AND/OR PERSONALITY-ORIENTED VIOLENCE

This is admittedly a catchall category which includes cases of political violence which are primarily oriented toward a particular issue or set of issues, individuals, or groups. Not included herein is violence which is primarily primordial in character or part of a wider revolutionary movement. As with the previously discussed categories, this delineation is necessarily arbitrary inasmuch as the particular issues involved might have religious, racial, or ideological coloration. However, we are again analyzing these cases in terms of the primary thrust of the acts of violence, accepting the fact that there may be ancillary motives or ideological support. This particular type of violence is subdivided into three categories: student activities, electoral politics, and economic and social issues such as political strikes for government reforms, land reform conflicts, or ghetto disputes. The variety of student violence often appears endless to the older generation, with targets including other students, the university administration, the government and its policies, foreign entrepreneurs and regimes, and numerous others. Issues have run the full gamut from university to national and international policies. Nor do targets and issues appear to differ greatly across the world, although the emphasis may vary from place to place. For example, William Hanna found that in Black Africa the content of student criticisms could be broken down into four categories: the university, emphasizing such issues as personal freedom; the university and the regime, including problems of academic freedom and financial support; the regime, ranging from particular government programs to style of rule; and international "aggressors," underlining Third World issues such as imperialism.[5] Countries experiencing student-oriented violence are listed in Table 1–5.

In Europe the major underpinnings to student violence have been ideological insofar as the violence involved attacks upon regimes or power structures of industrial societies and pragmatic insofar as the violence involved attacks upon inadequate and antiquated systems of secondary and higher education. In Latin America student violence has involved both domestic and international issues, including policies of military regimes and the activities of foreign "imperialists." In the United States, student-associated violence has been related primarily to the war in Indo-China, civil rights causes, and demands for changes in university policies.

Although students often publicly justify the need for violence to achieve goals and although the rhetoric of a small student minority is often apparently revolutionary, the levels of conflict (in terms of deaths and injuries) initiated by the students themselves have been comparatively low. Demonstrations and sabotage have been directed against property, but rarely have student violence targets been oriented toward personal injury.

---

[5] Hanna, 1971, p. 178–81. The entire issue of the *Annals of the American Academy* in which the essay appears is given over to an excellent survey of student protest in the United States and abroad. Also see Silverstein, 1970, and Altbach, 1970.

Table 1–5   Postwar or Post-Independence Student-Oriented Violence

Africa	Asia	Europe	Latin America	Middle East & North Africa
Congo (B)	Indonesia	France	Mexico	Egypt
Congo (K)	Burma	West Germany	Uruguay	Turkey
Tanzania	Thailand	Netherlands	Argentina	Lebanon
Kenya	Japan	United Kingdom	Colombia	Algeria
Nigeria	Korea	Czechoslovakia	Cuba	Morocco
Senegal	S. Vietnam	Italy	Bolivia	Sudan
Ethiopia	China (C)	Belgium	Brazil	Syria
Dahomey	Ceylon	Spain	Peru	Iran
Ivory Coast	Philippines		Guatemala	Libya
Ghana	India		Panama	
Gabon	Singapore		Dominican Republic	
Mauritus	Malaysia			
Upper Volta				
Uganda				
South Africa				

On the other hand, governments have met student activities with considerably greater force, resulting in death and injury in Burma, Pakistan, Japan, the United States, and fifty other countries. In the developing world in particular governments have seen student protest as a danger to their own survival. Student involvement in the overthrow of authority in Cuba, Turkey, and Korea has not gone unnoticed, and one leader has commented that, "We do not intend to sit idly by and see these institutions . . . continue to be centres of anti-government activities." [6] Often ill-organized

[6] Hanna, 1971, p. 179.

Table 1–6   Postwar or Post-Independence Electoral Violence

Africa	Asia	Europe	Latin America	Middle East & North Africa
Congo (K)	Philippines	Italy	Mexico	Lebanon
Lesotho	Burma	United States	Colombia	Libya
Dahomey	S. Vietnam		Venezuela	Syria
Sierra Leone	Japan		Argentina	
Zambia	S. Korea		Bolivia	
Somalia	Pakistan		Brazil	
Senegal	India		Costa Rica	
Nigeria			Panama	
Tanzania			Dominican Republic	
Upper Volta			Haiti	
			Guyana	

for extra-legal conflict, ill-armed, and at times seemingly bent upon violent policies dysfunctional to their stated aims, student movements rarely have been able to compete effectively against the establishment. Ironically, where student movements have been most successful in achieving change, they were dependent upon the cooperation of a simultaneously anti-government military establishment.

In many developing states low-level violence has become a "normal" part of political campaigning. Thus a Somali Prime Minister was able to remark that elections had been honest and fair, despite the fact that, "Naturally, there were incidents in several places and a total of 25 persons, unfortunately, lost their lives during the elections and its preceding campaigns." [7] During elections attacks are made upon candidates, followers, and party leaders. Even in such cases, however, the numbers injured or killed usually have been relatively small and do not appear to have a major impact upon the political system.

A wide variety of specific economic and social issues have become the focal points of emotional political causes leading to violent reactions against opponents or authority. In urban areas such issues have included government policies on housing, food, services, police power, and a wide range of other problems. Violence also has developed through political strikes and demonstrations; conflicts with the police and the military during riots; looting, sniping, and attacks upon chosen "enemies" such as landlords, government officials, and so forth. Examples are multitudinous: ghetto riots in United States, India, or Latin America; food riots in India and Pakistan; government-organized political demonstrations in pre-Nasser Egypt; conflict between two cities in Southern Italy over the placement of bureaucratic power; and numerous others.

In rural areas political violence has erupted over another variety of issues, ranging from land tenure, tax policies, and actions of particular local officials to administrative policies on land, water, forestry, and police powers. For example, rural conflict in northeast Thailand in the 1960s, while partially revolutionary in context, was related to a full panoply of complaints from treatment by government officials through neglect of local needs to regional loyalties. In the Philippines, parts of Vietnam, Bolivia, and prewar Burma violence tended to be related most commonly to land problems. Local issues such as cattle and land ownership have influenced conflict in various parts of Africa. Table 1–7 summarizes the types of violence we have discussed heretofore.

7 *African Research Bulletin,* 1969 (April 1–30), p. 1378.

Table 1–7   Percentages of Types of Violence in Postwar,
Post-Independence Nations *

Region	Number	Primor-dial	Sepa-ratist	Revolu-tionary	Coup	Student/Electoral
Africa	35	63%	25%	8%	71%	54%
Asia	19	74%	46%	63%	42%	74%
Latin America	23	8%	4%	25%	52%	73%
Middle East & North Africa	16	56%	25%	56%	75%	62%
Europe	30	27%	13%	13%	3%	33%

* This and other tables in this chapter were compiled from African Research Bulletin, Asian Re-
corder, Middle East Record, Facts on File, Encyclopedia Americana, and individual country
studies.

SUMMARY

A number of conclusions can be drawn from this categorization of political violence.

1. While religious and ethnic violence seems to be on the wane in Europe and Latin America, it still appears to be prevalent in Afro-Asia and North America.

2. Ideological and coup-oriented violence has been at somewhat low levels in Western Europe but is important elsewhere and particularly high in Afro-Asia. It should be noted that of the four events having the highest death counts in the postwar period, three were largely ideologically based —Vietnam, the Chinese Civil War and its aftermath, and the elimination of the Communists in Indonesia in 1965. The other case was primordial—the massacres accompanying the separation of India and Pakistan.

3. Political violence is rarely related to only one factor, and large-scale violence in particular usually results from a complex interrelationship of issues. States found in one category of conflict will usually appear in another. The number of types of violence may not relate to the intensity of conflict.

4. Coups are essentially nonexistent in Western democratic and most totalitarian systems. They are most prevalent in newly independent states and it is there that the greatest violence occurs.

5. The number of cases of student and electoral violence is very high, but casualties have remained comparatively low.

Violence has always cloaked itself in the garments of some means of making it legitimate. In defense of violence, man has insisted that he was provoked beyond human endurance; he has stated that he was not responsible by reason of insanity; he has pointed out that he acted only in self-defense; he has claimed that honor and manhood required violent response; he has maintained that he never intended to produce the outcome that occurred; he has said that what he did was for the ultimate good of society; and he has felt, if not said, that his actions were inescapably necessary given the situation in which he found himself.

Elton B. McNeil (1966, p. 155)

THE JUSTIFICATION AND RHETORIC OF VIOLENCE

2

Violence as an act may or may not be justified in systematic terms, but political violence usually is rationalized in terms sufficiently concrete to allow us to analyze its form and content. Efforts to legitimize political violence in the postwar era have been based upon a wide range of justifications, some religious and racial, others founded upon systematic secular ideologies, and still others demanding violence as a solution to specific social ills. This chapter is an effort to classify the basic forms of articulating the need for political violence and their influence on the political process. Five categories are considered, although these are not to be conceived of as all inclusive: (1) racial and religious, (2) ideological, (3) anti-colonial, (4) specific issue-oriented, and (5) coup violence. Although these categories overlap, they are intended to delineate the primary bases for the call to political violence. Thus, in some parts of the world anti-colonialism may have racial or religious overtones just as in the United States racially oriented violence often has revolved around specific grievances. Nevertheless, it appears possible to carve out the core of justification from the myriad of roots.

RACIAL AND RELIGIOUS VIOLENCE

The call to violence on the basis of race or religion has considerably less universality today than in the past. The Crusades, religious wars of Europe, American attacks upon Indians, anti-Jewish pogroms in Eastern Europe, and Hitler's campaign against the Jews are but examples of acts of violence which had their racially or religiously oriented apologists. In many of these cases princes, rulers, religious leaders, and the populace were united in the manner in which they justified their acts. Recent cries for violence based upon such primordial causes have found less support from national leaders and efforts have been made to clothe such statements in more "acceptable" terms. It is no longer "proper," except in international affairs, to crusade against a particular primordial group, and as a result the articulators of this kind of violence are more and more to be found among fringe groups and depressed minorities. Even here, those seeking to legitimate violence can be divided among those who blatantly call for conflict ("kill whitey" or "liquidate the Jews" or "destroy the Ibo"); those who clothe racial or religious justification in more general political terms (e.g., statements in the India-Pakistan conflict and much of U.S. racial politics); and, finally, those who personally decry violence while expressing "understanding" for why others chose such alternatives. Each tends to legitimize the use of force.

Examples of justifications of violence founded upon race or religion have arisen regularly, if less frequently in the postwar years, on every continent, although Latin America and Western Europe have been somewhat less prone to such statements. Only two cases of religiously oriented justification of political conflict appear to have been important in the postwar period. First, anti-communist crusades in the West have, in rare cases, employed religious demands for the destruction of "Godless Communism." Although these pleas normally have been nonviolent, some fringe groups have cited Christianity as an excuse for violence. The second example is more blatant: the Catholic-Protestant conflict in Northern Ireland where cries against the "Papists" and "Paisleyites" have often been violent in tone. In this region violence has been justified in terms of historic animosities, charges of bias on the part of the authorities (including the constabulary), economic and social conditions which were not changing under peaceful pressure, and antipathy toward outside interference. (See Chapter 4.) These long-term divisions in the population provided traditional emotional support to direct action. In the words of a song sung by the Protestants when confronting the British troops: "With heart and hand, and sword and shield, we'll guard old Derry Walls." [1]

Religiously-based violence has been far more prevalent in states in the earlier phases of nation-building when communal rivalries in general have been closer to the surface. In Africa the line of conflict has often been at the point where expanding Islam has come into contact with Christian and other "kafir" populations. In these areas religious divisions became entangled in both tribal and economic-political antagonisms. Violence has developed at high levels where communal groups have demanded autonomy and have been refused by a regime in power of a different faith (for example, Chad and the Sudan).

Similar claims for autonomy or independence by religious groups have

---

[1] Quoted in Hastings, 1970, p. 184.

been the foundation for conflict in Asia as well. As in Africa, these demands normally are not simply religious in nature but combine both other communal and economic-political rivalries with religious divisions. Violence has asserted itself in such rivalries in Burma, Indonesia, the Philippines, and Thailand, where groups such as the Karens, Ambonese, Moros, and Thai-Moslems have found members who have claimed that violence was the only means of gaining religious freedom.

The fear and suspicion of being ruled by another religion helped to generate extremely violent communal conflict in the massacres that followed the separation of India and Pakistan. Again, historic antagonisms led to not unfounded fears among both the Moslem minorities in India and the Hindu minorities in Pakistan that they would be attacked. At the same time members of the majority group made emotional, and at times economic and political, demands that the state be cleansed of adherents to the other faith. As the massacres developed, cries for vengeance for the deaths of co-religionists led to further violence until perhaps half a million were killed. In this case the leaders of both countries called for peace and worked to quiet their people, but those at lower levels were not of the same notion. As a Moslem pamphlet quoted in a strongly pro-Indian book allegedly proclaimed,

> *The Sword of Islam must be shining in the heavens and will subdue all evil designs. . . . Be ready to take your swords. Think you, Muslims, why we are under the* kafirs *today. . . . O* kafir! *Do not be proud and happy. Your doom is not far and general massacre will come.*[2]

Religiously based anti-Communism has also been employed as a justification for violence, particularly in Burma, Indonesia, and the Philippines. In Burma, the government backed a campaign among Buddhists, Christians, and Moslems against the indigenous Communist movement. In this case it was decided to fit the demands for violence to the religion in question. The Buddhist anti-Communist pamphlets and speeches played down violence while the Moslem statements reminded readers of Middle Eastern examples of violence displayed against nonbelievers, with hints that the same activities might be employed against local enemies of the faith. The Christians were found in between, the strongest assertion being,

> *If you happen to be helping the Communists in your local area, be they Burman, Shan, Karen, Kachin, Chin, Arakanese, Mon or any of our races in Burma, or helping those who are helping or joining forces with the Communists you have then betrayed Christ.*[3]

[2] Das Khosla, n.d., pp. 52–53.

[3] *The Burning Question*, n.d., back cover. For an analysis of this campaign see von der Mehden, 1960.

Finally, there have been justifications of violence against co-religionists who have not been properly orthodox. This type of conflict has happened particularly in Islam as the Dar ul Islam in Indonesia and various sects in the Middle East either have forcibly attempted to bring fellow Moslems into line or have attacked those perceived as backsliders.

A totally separate conflict in which religion has played an important if often ambiguous role is to be found in the Arab-Israeli dispute. The rhetoric of the conflict usually has carefully skirted religious issues inasmuch as anti-Semitism as such is difficult to develop as a point of antagonism within the Middle East, given the Semitic origin of all contesting parties. Instead, the Arabs have called for war against Israel and local Jews on the basis of anti-imperialist and anti-Zionist arguments stressing Arab unity and Israeli aggression; for their part, the Israelis have based their actions on the necessity of defending their state and people. Thus, Nasser promised that, "When the Arab nation once again reverts to its unity with a view of destroying the influence of imperialism as well as the imperialistic stooges, we must destroy Zionism," [4] and an Israeli translation of a Palestinian liberation movement pamphlet read,

> The liberation action is not only the removal of an armed imperialist base; but, more important—it is the destruction of a society. [Our] armed violence will be expressed in many ways. In addition to the destruction of the military force of the Zionist occupying state, it will also be turned toward the destruction of the means of life of Zionist society in all their forms—industrial, agricultural and financial.[5]

Israelis have followed a policy of threatening retaliation and displaying force, as illustrated by Levi Ishkol's threat prior to the Six-Day War:

> The firm and persistent stand we have taken on behalf of our rights have strengthened the wariness among our neighbors that they will not be able to prevail against us in open combat. . . . If they try to sow unrest in our border—unrest will come to theirs.[6]

Nevertheless, although terms such as "destroy," "eliminate," and the "liquidation of the agent rulers" appear rather regularly in Arab documents, and although Jews in Arab lands have not always been treated kindly since the establishment of Israel, religion as such has not been the normal base

---

[4] *Middle East Record*, 1961, p. 182.

[5] Quoted in *Israelis Reply*, 1970. Statements similar to this one from an Israeli publication abound in Arab liberation movement pronouncements.

[6] Quoted in Draper, 1967, p. 247.

for these demands for violence. Arab leaders usually have noted that their target is not the Jewish people or their religion. It has been a different story outside the area, where anti-Israeli positions often have been based on anti-Semitic attitudes.

Turning from religious to racial justifications of violence, we should note that spokesmen proposing violence as a solution to racial problems have appeared in numerous Afro-Asian states including Rwanda, Burma, Nigeria, India, Pakistan, and Kenya. Some pronouncements have been clearly violent in tone, with specific demands to kill or injure opponents, while others have been more carefully camouflaged. In the developing world written statements formulating the necessity for violence have not always reached the outside world. The most numerous and articulate justifications for racial violence presently available have thus come from white and black racists in the United States—a consideration which calls to mind the often neglected fact that primarily racial or ethnic justifications of violence have not been restricted to the developing world.

In the United States four primary justifications of racial violence may be distinguished: vengeance against past or present injustices; defense of the group; the cleansing of society of undesirable elements; and the achievement of desired social change. Some of these justifications have been found in the rhetoric of racists elsewhere both in the West and in developing nations.

VIOLENCE AS REVENGE

Violence has been demanded by some black militants in the United States on the grounds that past and present ill-treatment by the dominant community requires retribution. This argument was also used in the developing world as well, where, for example, the Hutu fought against former Tutsi domination in Rwanda and various Southeast Asians have decried Chinese economic control of their lives and have launched pogroms from time to time. But black militants in the United States have been the most articulate spokesmen for violence as retribution for past wrongs committed against oppressed people over the centuries. The following statements illustrate different reactions to such treatment.

> RAP BROWN: *No one can tell me who my enemy is and I know how to kill him. . . . When I get mad, I'm going out and look for a honky, and I'm going to take out 400 years' worth of dues on him.*[7]

[7] Quoted in Geltman, 1970, p. 32.

ROBERT WILLIAMS: *When a brutally oppressed and dehumanized people are denied the peaceful channels through which to activate redress, and when their peaceful petitions are answered with ruthless violence, the only recourse left to them is to meet violence with violence.*[8]

VIOLENCE AS SELF-DEFENSE

Blacks and whites, both here and abroad, have asserted the need for violence as a means of self-defense against other racial groups. Such self-defense is necessary, it is argued, because those in power are unwilling or unable to defend the group, if in fact they are not leading the attack. The following are examples of a very common position:

NSRP SPOKESMAN: *If it takes killing to get the negroes out of the white man's streets and to protect our constitutional rights, I say, yes, kill them.*[9]

MALCOLM X: *We assert the right of self-defense by whatever means necessary, and reserve the right of maximum retaliation against our racist oppressors, no matter what the odds against us are. From here on in, if we must die anyway, we will die fighting back and we will not die alone. We intend to see that our racist oppressors also get a taste of death.*[10]

HUTU SPOKESMAN: *We are expected to defend ourselves. The only way to go about it is to paralyse the Tutsi. How? They must be killed.*[11]

BLACK MILITANT: *Guerrilla warfare is the black man's answer to the white man's final solution. . . . The white man in this country has almost decided on genocide as the only way to silence the black man's revolt and as Rap Brown puts it so eloquently we don't intend to walk meekly to the gas chambers.*[12]

VIOLENCE AS SOCIAL PURGE

Through the centuries various races and religions have been considered so dangerous or undesirable that there have been those who have wanted to eliminate them from the community. Of course, the most noted recent example of this policy was the German liquidation of several million Jews, but other examples can be cited. Both blacks and whites have justified

[8] Robert F. Williams, "For 'Effective Self Defense,'" in Broderick and Meier, 1965, pp. 332–33.

[9] Quoted in "The Rhetoric of Vilification and Violence," in Kirkham, Levy, and Crotty, 1970, p. 346.

[10] Breitman, 1965, pp. 76–77.

[11] Quoted in Lemarchand, 1970, pp. 223–24.

[12] Quoted in Rowan, 1967.

violence against other groups on this basis. Thus the fact that blacks in the United States have been defined as of "criminal character" serves as a justification of violence by law enforcement officers. White racists have talked more in terms of eliminating blacks or Jews, whereas blacks have charged that the nation has needed cleansing of undesirable elements.

> ROBERT SHELTON OF THE KU KLUX KLAN: *The only scourge in America today is the leper Jew. Kill him, and we have no more trouble about Communism, Negroes, money, taxes, economy, or political crooks in office or getting along with the rest of the world. Kill him economically, politically, and socially. Do THIS and the white race of all the earth will owe Americans an undying debt of gratitude.*[13]

> BLACK PANTHER: *America, you will be cleansed by fire, by blood, by death. We who perform your ablution must step up our burning—bigger and better fires, one flame for all America, an all-American flame; we must step up our looting—loot, until we storm your last hoarding place, till we trample your last stolen jewel into ashes beneath our naked black feet; we must step up our sniping—until the last pig is dead, shot to death with his own gun and the bullets in his guts that he had meant for the people. . . .*[14]

VIOLENCE FOR SOCIAL CHANGE

Finally, racial violence has been justified as the only possible means to gain necessary social and political change. Black and white militants have declared that the "power structure" can be brought to its knees only by force. Thus the formerly exiled revolutionary Robert F. Williams argued in 1964 that only by violence could black America achieve freedom:

> *The most noble of mankind must surely aspire for a human level of endeavor, wherein mankind can establish a utopian society divested of brute force and violence. The irony of this great dream is that if it is at all possible, it is possible only through the medium of violence. It is possible only through Revolution.*[15]

IDEOLOGICAL VIOLENCE Secular ideologies have been key elements in the explanation of political violence during the twentieth century. Nazism called for both international conflict to achieve German greatness and domestic liquidation of Jews and others to establish German purity, while Marxism-Leninism presented the necessary theoretic foundations to legitimize the violent overthrow of estab-

[13] Kirkham, Levy, and Crotty, 1970, pp. 345–46.

[14] *Ibid.*, p. 348.

[15] Williams, *op. cit.*, p. 326.

lished regimes. In the postwar era Nazism is no longer employed to legitimize violence except by miniscule fringe groups, but the successors of Marx and Lenin are still debating the necessity of conflict to achieve goals. At the same time, a welter of nascent "ideologies" have risen to justify violent actions against the state. Some of these ideologies are linked to Marxism-Leninism and deserve brief notice.

Although traditional Marxism noted the need for conflict in order to successfully overcome the enemies of the people, it saw violence in instrumental terms and placed no emphasis whatever on mere killing, maiming, and the infliction of pain.[16]

In the postwar era the Communist world has largely bifurcated with regard to the theoretical need for violence to achieve goals. For simplicity's sake these views may be divided into the Soviet-supported contention that there are "many roads to Socialism" and the Maoist assessment that violence normally will be necessary.

Contemporary Soviet theory has not eliminated violence as one road to power, although it certainly has diminished the central role of violence in internal wars. Force is no longer envisioned as mandatory for overcoming the capitalist countries. At least since 1959, it has been conceded and even stressed that there now exist nonviolent ways of gaining preponderance over the dominating classes. This shift can in part be explained by the fact that the Soviets have been dealing largely with European states where the parliamentary system does not seem readily vulnerable to internal use of force. Thus, Communist spokesmen in Western European states have been even more circumspect than their Soviet allies in discussing the role of violence in Communist theory and have tended to emphasize the "many roads to Socialism."

Chinese Communist theory, while not denying the possibility of a peaceful road to power, centers strongly on the need for violence. As Mao once commented, "political power grows out of the barrel of a gun." The most noted Chinese statement appeared in 1960 when it was declared that,

> The capitalist-imperialist system absolutely will not crumble of itself. It will be pushed over by the proletarian revolution within the imperialist country concerned, and the national revolution in the colonial and semi-colonial countries.[17]

16 Black and Thornton, 1965, p. 38.
17 Ibid., p. 412.

It is fundamentally the growing differences over the role of violence that lies at the root of theoretical differences between Moscow and Peking. "Independent" Communists such as Tito and Castro also have partaken in this debate. The Yugoslavs were the first to argue that it is possible to achieve success through peaceful means—at least in the advanced nations, but there appears to be some doubt about the efficacy of this alternative for the developing nations. Facing a somewhat different situation, Castro's declarations have fallen between the Soviet and Maoist positions. Violence has long been a part of Latin American domestic politics and has been especially prevalent in Cuba and those states (Colombia, Venezuela, and Bolivia) where Castro and his followers have attempted to influence political life. Perhaps one of the best expressions of Castro's views on the role of violence appeared in the Final Proclamation of the Latin American Solidarity Organization (LASO) at a conference in Havana in 1967. Three of the twenty parts read:

1. That it is the right and the duty of the peoples of Latin America to make revolution.
2. That armed revolutionary struggle is the primary path of the revolution in Latin America.
3. That guerrillas, as the embryo of the armies of liberation, are the most effective means of initiating and developing revolutionary struggle in the *majority of our countries*.[18]

SUBNATIONAL "IDEOLOGIES"

A multitude of political programs have arisen in the postwar world which either have not received national support or have remained so unsystematic in their formulations as to bring into question their place as ideologies. These concepts have included "Négritude," "Aprismo," "Perónismo," "MANIPOL-USDEK," "Arab Socialism," and the ideas of the young revolutionaries of the West. Most of these "ideologies" have been eclectic in their heritage, owing much both to Marxism and to indigenous nationalism.

Not all of these subnational ideologies contain elements of violence and, in fact, most of the post-independence concepts of the new elites have not supported the domestic use of force to achieve goals. This does not mean that they have eschewed the possible use of violence, but that, unlike the Communists, they do not normally accept the use of violence as a doctrinal element.

We should also note the special case of younger articulators of violence in the United States, Western Europe, and Japan in recent years. In some

---

[18] Quoted in Mathews, 1970, p. 288; italics added.

cases, particularly student groups that are strongly centered in Leninism, Maoism, or even Marcusianism, a reasonably coherent ideological base can be identified. But most of the "little groups" in Western Europe, as well as almost the entire student movement in the United States is not only without ideology but often downright hostile to it.

As one examines the considerable verbal (and musical!) outpourings of these groups, it is possible to delineate several justifications for political violence. Among the wide variety of such justifications have been:

1. Violence is Romantic To some, violent acts appear to offer a satisfaction of their own, aside from the impact they might have on the political system. As one self-described "conservative radical" commented, it gave him "a little satisfaction when the Bank of America burns down or IBM blows up." [19]

2. Violence is Necessary for Change As in the case of racial violence, the radical elements of the New Left have argued that the only way to get the system to change is to force it into action. The ideal society can be brought about only through violence because the power structure is unwilling to permit itself to be reformed by other means. As two militants argued,

> *In death-directed Amerika there is only one way to a life of love and free-dom: to attack and destroy the forces of death and exploitation and to build a just society—revolution.*
>
> *Peaceful demonstrations just don't work. Whatever violence the left may do is not as violent as that of the establishment.* [20]

3. The System is Immoral Revolutionaries who take this line of approach almost appear to be repeating the words of Mussolini, who proclaimed that there was "a violence that liberates, and a violence that enslaves . . . a violence that is moral and a violence that is immoral." [21] Because the system itself is immoral, it is a moral act to destroy it. "What is the burning of a bank compared to the founding of a bank?" radicals ask, and answer with the declaration that "There is more violence in the ROTC building than there is in blowing it up." [22] Almost all defenders of violent policies, whether on the national or the international level, have

[19] *San Francisco Sunday Examiner & Chronicle,* April 5, 1970.

[20] *Time,* March 23, 1970, p. 11.

[21] Quoted in Demaris, 1970, p. 227.

[22] *San Francisco Sunday Chronicle and Examiner,* April 5, 1970.

asserted that their acts were moral, or at least that the immorality of the enemy was of such a magnitude as to justify violence. God is rarely considered to be on the other side.

4. *Violence Dramatizes*   Violence is considered a necessary tactic for dramatizing to the outside world the immorality of those in power. Without it, the people would continue to support the established regime, largely unaware of what is being perpetrated. It is also necessary to show the outside world the power and seriousness of those leading the struggle. As a student stated,

> *I don't think the working class people of this country will ever take the student seriously until students become people again, and come off the campus, and be willing to kill and die for their [i.e., the people's] freedom.*[23]

5. *Violence is Vengeance*   Next, there are those who have committed acts of violence as retribution for past injustices, specific or general. As one black militant wrote, "To America: I'm playing heads-up murder. . . . Dynamite is my response to your justice."[24]

6. *Violence is Needed to Destroy the System* Revolutionaries often stress the necessity of destroying the system in order to establish one more to their liking. In the words of Eldridge Cleaver, "I think the people's war should be escalated in terms of revolutionary violence against the system, specifically designed to destroy the system."[25]

Emotional appeals to violence from the radical left have been mirrored by similar statements from the right. Indeed it seems, at least superficially, that in postwar America the right has been more articulate, more prepared to publicize its call for violence, and more fully reported by the press. In Europe, on the other hand, articulate young spokesmen have appeared at both ends of the spectrum. While both the right and the left employ the rhetoric of violence, differences can be seen in content of their respective statements. The rhetoric from the right has been racist and nationalist in tone while the left has displayed internationalist, Marxist, and anarchist leanings. However, racism has not been monopolized by the right, as can be seen in black nationalist references to anti-white violence, which have in turn been supported by sections of the New Left. The following statements by left and right display at least some superficial similarities. The first is a

[23] Kirkham, Levy, and Crotty, 1970, p. 349.
[24] *Time*, March 23, 1970, p. 9.
[25] Quoted in Schanche, 1970, p. 208.

statement made at a Ku Klux Klan meeting about a church bombing that killed four little black children; the second is a statement by a Black Muslim named Allah or 13X.

> If they can find those fellows, they ought to pin medals on them. It wasn't no shame they was killed. . . . Why? Because when I go out to kill rattlesnakes, I don't make no difference between little rattlesnakes and big rattlesnakes. . . .[26]

> We're going to kill the cops and all the white people—women and children, too. We're going to start a blood bath now, and if we don't get our share of poverty funds, blood will flow.[27]

ANTI-COLONIAL VIOLENCE

Anti-colonial movements have produced some of the most eloquent and emotional justifications for the necessity of political violence in the postwar era, although most leaders of independence movements have not seen the need to employ raw force in order to achieve their goals and would not agree with Frantz Fanon that "the colonized man finds his freedom in and through violence." Anti-colonial movements have produced both those who have spoken in terms more violent than their actions and those who have led bloody revolts against the metropolitan power in colonies such as Indo-China, Algeria, Indonesia, Aden, and Mozambique. We should, therefore, divide the statements of the anti-colonialists into those where the rhetoric is not reflected in the policies and those where the rhetoric reflects the need to use more than peaceful means to achieve independence.

The vast majority of Black African and South Asian nationalist leaders have been committed to nonviolent programs, and many have publicly referred to the teachings of Gandhi. In fact, the policies of the United Kingdom and France in most of their colonies were such as to negate the need for violence to achieve independence. Thus, the statements of Kwame Nkrumah, Félix Houphouet-Boigny, Mohandas K. Gandhi, Jawaharlal Nehru, Benjamin Azikiwe, and other Afro-Asian leaders normally did not include a call to bloody conflict during the decade prior to the independence of their respective countries. Few anti-colonial movements have been so influenced by the necessity of violence as to base their policies on the Algerian FLN (National Liberation Front) principle that "negotiations follow the

[26] Quoted in Wolfgang, 1966, p. 142.

[27] Kirkham, Levy, and Crotty, 1970, p. 348.

all out struggle against a pitiless enemy, it never precedes it." Nevertheless, nationalist leaders often feared that the colonial power would not provide freedom soon enough, and there were periods when the rhetoric became more violent, particularly in nationalist newspapers.

Among nationalist leaders, the most frequent and bitter justifications of political violence have been articulated by those participating in colonial wars. Reasons for violence have been largely based upon demands for freedom and independence, allegedly blocked by colonial governments and their supporters. Calls for violence might appear in clandestine pamphlets, on the walls of buildings, in interviews or publications produced in foreign lands, or by any other means open to those leading the struggle for independence. Eloquent justifications for violent policies have come from Indo-China, Indonesia, North Africa, and Portuguese Africa, as well as from radical spokesmen in countries where leading nationalists have sought peaceful change. Examples of these cries for violence are multitudinous, but the following may provide the flavor of their rhetoric:

Ho Chi Minh: *Compatriots! Rise up! Men and women, old and young, regardless of creeds, political parties or nationalities, all the Vietnamese must stand up to fight the French colonialists to save the fatherland. Those who have rifles will use their rifles; those who have swords will use their swords; those who have no swords will use spades, hoes or sticks. Everyone must endeavor to oppose the colonialists and save his country.*[28]

Anonymous: *Up till then, our struggle was on the plane of negotiation. It was only after exhausting all possibilities of a peaceful solution that we decided to take up arms. We are now sure that this is the only means by which to convince the Portuguese people in Mozambique to get out, to give back what belongs to us, to restore us to our land.*[29]

Algerian FLN Platform: *It is a national struggle to destroy the anarchic regime of colonization and not a religious war. It is a step forward in the historic direction of humanity and not a return toward feudalism.*[30]

Even after independence is achieved there are those who believe that the last vestiges of colonialism have not been eradicated and that force remains necessary in order to achieve full freedom from the imperialists.

---

[28] Ho Chi Minh, 1960–62, III, 81–82.

[29] Quoted from "Voices of Revolution," 1966, p. 123. Another statement from the same source declared that, "We have nothing to lose. Existence itself has no meaning in a *regime* of *servitude*. We have nothing to lose but the chains that destroy our dignity."

[30] Quoted in Gillespie, 1960, p. 135.

On the metropolitan side, anti-colonial wars and violence can lead to extreme demands that violence be committed against "rebels," "terrorists," and "guerrillas." The bloody histories of torture and inhumanity in Algeria and the Portuguese African territories are stark examples of this pattern of escalation. It can perhaps be summed up in an anonymous statement by colonists attempting to discourage both Algerian independence and French desires for negotiation: "Everywhere the traitors are beginning to tremble. They know that blows of the patriots will not spare them. Coffins are waiting for them in Paris as well as in Algiers."[31]

SPECIFIC ISSUE- ORIENTED VIOLENCE

Conflict related to specific issues may also generate justifications for the use of violence to achieve political ends. Specific issues may include unpopular domestic policies such as draft laws in the United States, agricultural programs in France, squatter rights in Indonesia, the place of an administrative center in Italy, taxation rules in Nigeria, or high bride prices in Africa. The foreign policy of the government or even the policies of foreign government also may bring violence. Thus violence has arisen in Australia and the United Kingdom in opposition to South African apartheid; in Colombia in opposition to American economic and cultural "imperialism"; in Latin America in opposition to the visit of an American Vice President; in the United States in opposition to Soviet Jewish policy; and in Burma in opposition to the Chinese Cultural Revolution. There also have been violent manifestations of antagonism toward the foreign policy of indigenous governments in the United States with regard to Vietnam programs, in Britain with regard to arms shipments to South Africa, and in Lebanon with regard to purported government softness on Israel. Specific problems not initially involving the state may develop into political questions when violence is experienced. The variety of such cases includes everything from "commodity riots" in the United States, strikes in Europe, and even soccer games in Latin America.

The justification for this type of violence normally is presented after the fact, for the character of these situations usually is not such as to lead one beforehand to propose open conflict as the solution. Indeed, this type of violence often develops from counteraction by authorities to largely peaceful demonstrations.

When violence does accompany confrontation over such issue-oriented questions, the justifications are, in most cases, comparatively simple, pragmatic, and unencumbered by systematic explanations—unless of course the

[31] Quoted in Bocca, 1968, pp. 48–49.

issue is or can be made to be part of a larger ideological conflict. For example, violence may be justified if:

1. It is considered necessary to dramatize the issue in order to aid group morale or bring the issue to the attention of the public;
2. It can be argued that violence took place only as a defense against authorities who were illegally attempting to disrupt basically peaceful demonstrators who reacted violently only out of anger at outrages or in order to protect themselves;
3. Violent action was necessary because the government or other opposition could not be convinced to change its policies by peaceful persuasion;
4. Those who are ideologically oriented see an escalation of confrontation as a way to radicalize workers, students, or others embroiled in the dispute.

COUP VIOLENCE The final justification of violence we will be considering here relates to statements made by non-revolutionary coup groups in order to legitimize the need to overthrow the regime in power. Here the major spokesman is usually a military figure. The characteristic situation is one in which there is no call for violence; indeed, the hope is often expressed that the operation will be peaceful. The military may have certain enemies that it wishes to bring to justice but the coup leaders normally do not have the sort of group targets that the primordial, ideological, or anti-colonial spokesmen attack.

Coup-justifying statements tend to be pragmatic rather than ideological in tone. They may stress the need to "get a few good chaps together," as in the Pakistani coup of 1958, or the idea that "we have no faith in the people who were ruling us," as was stated during a Zambian coup. More often than not the need for a coup is presented in a list of charges against the opposition, accompanied by a plea for law and order. An excellent example of this kind of justification was produced by the leaders of the 1971 coup in Uganda, one of the more violent overthrows. Alluding to corruption among ministers and top civil servants, arbitrary laws and officials, heavy taxes, high food prices, the failure to hold elections in eight years, the wealthy growing richer while they talked socialism, and the promotion of the former Prime Minister's tribesmen in the civil and military services, the statement pleaded,

We all want unity in Uganda and we don't want bloodshed. Everybody in Uganda knows that the matters mentioned above appear to us to lead to bloodshed only.[32]

[32] *African Research Bulletin,* January 1–31, 1971, pp. 1993–94.

SUMMARY

We can identify at least five clear threads that run through public justifications of violence as a means of achieving political goals.

1. *Defense*—Violence is considered necessary to protect the group, particularly from the authorities. In some cases violence is a reaction to past or present threats to the group; in others, threats of violence are used by one group to warn others that future attacks will be met by violent responses.
2. *Vengeance*—Violence is demanded as retribution for past acts against the group.
3. *Necessity*—Violence is seen as the only means available for achieving desired goals. Conflict is defined as the only remaining avenue to success, and those who oppose the perpetrators of or spokesmen for violence are accused of intransigence.
4. *Immorality*—The opposition and its policies are perceived as immoral; all efforts to defeat the enemy are defined as moral acts.
5. *Destruction of the system*—Political violence for this purpose is rarely selective in its ultimate targets, although the specific act may be directed against a single individual, building, or other specific target. This sort of violence is not considered a tactic against a specific element in the system, but is, in Eldridge Cleaver's words, "designed to destroy the system."

Our examination of the justifications of violence leaves us to ask if there is any correlation between the rhetoric of violence and the extent of conflict within a given society. An appendix to a staff report of the National Commission on the Causes and Prevention of Violence accepts the relationship between rhetoric and violent action, arguing that, "The groups which foster a rhetoric of violence produce or attract members who are willing to resort to violent action." [33] The report then gives specific examples which it believes proves its case, including alleged violence involving the KKK and Black Panthers.

In a somewhat more sophisticated analysis Ted Gurr notes that

> *Slogans imbedded in revolutionary ideologies can be sufficiently explicit in their prescription of violence that their dissemination provides sufficient clues for violence, though it seems unlikely that such slogans can precipitate a wholly new, unfamiliar type of collective action. . . .*
>
> *A call to arms or appeals to traditions of political violence seem less effective as stimuli for violence than news of the occurrence of violence elsewhere, or at best are effective only in conjunction with such news.*[34]

---

[33] Kirkham, Levy, and Crotty, 1970, p. 355.

[34] Gurr, 1970, p. 227. At the same time Gurr presents the hypothesis that "The greater the number of representations of political violence in men's communication intake, the more likely they are to accept such violence as a mode of behavior." *Ibid.*, p. 231.

On a cross-national basis it would appear that there is no necessary relationship between the degree of aggressiveness of the rhetoric of violence and the extent of conflict that accompanies or follows it. In fact, there is almost an inverse relationship. Some spokesmen of the black and white militants and New Left revolutionaries of the postwar era have escalated the rhetoric of violence to new heights, calling for killing, looting, and the destruction of property. Yet the violence perpetrated by these groups has been at a relatively low level and has not precipitated extensive counteraction. A survey of high casualty events in countries such as Pakistan, India, Rwanda, Indonesia, and Nigeria evidences comparatively fewer public demands for violence. In these states, where rural literacy is usually low, the call to battle is probably issued more by word of mouth and less by public utterances.

"ESTABLISHMENT VIOLENCE"

3

It is clear that all state systems consider violence a normal element in the maintenance of domestic tranquility and the threat of violence—from the nightstick to capital punishment—a deterrent to deviant behavior. Violence, then, in certain forms and constrained by certain limits, is considered legitimate by all societies, whether democratic or not.

Nevertheless, considerable debate and polemical outpouring is increasingly associated with charges of establishment violence on the one hand and demands for greater attention to enforced law and order on the other.

This chapter seeks to analyze establishment violence employed to achieve more partisan political goals. In assessing this phenomenon, three areas will be emphasized: (1) governmental acts to curb "ordinary crime" when such acts are perceived as political; (2) obviously politically oriented establishment use of force; and (3) the rationale for the employment of force by authority for the achievement of political ends.

GOVERNMENTAL VIOLENCE AND "ORDINARY CRIME"

The matter of gathering data on the political acts of violence by established authorities is fraught with difficulties, as was mentioned early in this book. For example, area experts have told the author of assassinations of provincial, district, and village opponents which were not reported in the press in Brazil, Indonesia, Guatemala, China, Thailand, Nepal, Vietnam, and other countries. It is not possible to verify these reports and they can appear only as "judgmental assessments" in aggregate analysis.

A second problem of course is that of identifying when a known act of violence is carried out for political purposes. Certain acts defined as criminal obviously are politically motivated. Laws designed to muzzle public criticism of a regime fall into this category, as do laws dealing with conspiracies of all sorts, not just those designed to overthrow the political system.

The problem becomes even more complex when individuals are arrested, injured, or killed while committing an "accepted crime" (murder, riot, arson, property damage, kidnapping) in the process of carrying out a political act. Thus, are European, Japanese, or American students injured while destroying university property in a demonstration against government policy to be considered targets of establishment political repression or "criminals" who were hurt while committing an ordinary crime?

Violence used in halting "ordinary crime" when a political demonstration is not taking place usually is not considered political in nature. However, when it is claimed that police power has been employed unequally against citizens of the state or that the law has not defined all crimes equally, the use of violence to suppress crime quickly takes on a political dimension. Thus minorities in the United States have asserted that greater violence has been used against them in criminal cases than has been employed against the majority race. Specific uses of force may not be described as political, but arrests of blacks have been attacked as part of a political conspiracy. The high percentage of blacks arrested is perceived by many to be part of an effort by the establishment to keep them in a deprived status and "police brutality" has become a key political battle cry among both black and white opponents of the American system.[1]

Crime also may become political if it is perceived that crimes by different classes are treated with different sanctions by those in power. In the United States and Western Europe two examples come to mind. Business "crimes" (e.g., conspiracy in restraint of trade, pollution, dangerous or shoddy products, fraudulent practices) are considered by many of the young and minorities to be less vulnerable to government sanctions than are less harmful crimes committed by the poor. This perceived disparity has become a political issue which serves as a makeshift justification for a second type of "class crime." During recent years there has appeared what Morris Janowitz calls "commodity riots," in which blacks and other minorities have burned and looted ghetto stores, justifying their acts as retribution against the cheating and robbing of minorities practiced by both the specific stores and American business in general.[2]

---

[1] For a discussion of the role of police in crime and race relations, see Endleman, 1968.

[2] Morris Janowitz, "Patterns of Collective Racial Violence," in Graham and Gurr, 1969, pp. 412–44.

**POLITICAL
VIOLENCE**

The more obvious forms of establishment political violence can be considered under four classifications: (1) Attacks upon power contenders; (2) Efforts to instill unity or maintain order; (3) Quelling those expressing opposition to the regime where such individuals or groups are not of immediate danger to those in power and do not employ violent tactics; (4) Elimination of persons or groups considered "undesirable."

ATTACKS UPON POWER CONTENDERS

It has been a normal pattern through the centuries for those in power to use violence against possible contenders for their authority. In the past princes such as the Medicis or early Russian Tsars did away with dangerous rivals, at times including their own relatives; the Star Chamber or other private courts had political foes executed quietly; and civil wars were fought to gain control of the reins of power.

In more recent years, the interwar period was one of classic purges of the rivals of powerful leaders. In the mid-1920s Chiang Kai-shek moved against his opponents from the Chinese Communist Party and its supporters, killing large numbers and ultimately forcing the Communists into the hills of Yenan. In the following decade several purges took place in the totalitarian states. Adolph Hitler, once he achieved power, used the force of the state to eliminate his enemies from the old parties as well as possible contenders within the National Socialist Party. From Moscow in the same period Stalin unleashed the Great Purge—the use of "judicial assassination" to exile, jail, or execute thousands of opponents. Earlier another form of mass violence had been committed upon tens of thousands of Kulaks. Since World War II the elimination of elite power contenders by means of violence has continued to decline in the West, and even in Eastern Europe and the USSR jail sentences have come to replace more severe forms of violence. In the United States there have been charges of the elimination of opponents from the assassination of the Kennedys to the alleged complicity of authorities in the elimination of leaders of the Black Panther movement.

During the interwar period there were less spectacular examples of establishment violence against possible power contenders in Eastern Europe, the Middle East, and Latin America. Thus, the attempted assassination of the opposition newspaperman Carlos Lacerda of Brazil was laid at the door of the late President Vargas, although Lacerda could not be considered a major contender to power. Similarly, charges of government complicity in the assassination of popular opposition leader Gaitan of Colombia led to bloody riots and the new socialist government of Chile was accused—probably falsely—of having some role in the death of a former minister. On the whole, however, it should be noted that postwar Latin American states (with the prime exception of Cuba) usually have followed the policy of not killing the loser in coups or revolutions. On the other hand, there have been numerous allegations of quiet elimination of second- and third-line opponents in several countries including Haiti, the Dominican Republic, Colombia, Guatemala, and pre-Castro Cuba.

Afro-Asia has experienced the largest number of political assassinations or attempts in the postwar era, with the victims including leaders of Burma, Vietnam, Pakistan, India, Iraq, Syria, Egypt, Jordan, Yemen, Ceylon, and a majority of African states. Yet there have been few examples of proven "extra-legal" elimination of power contenders by those in control, although there have been charges of foreign efforts to kill off leaders of other states; known domestic cases include the execution of Patrice Lumumba, allegedly by the Congolese government, and the assassination of the leader of the Moslem Brotherhood in 1949 by Egyptian authorities after the death of Premier Nukrashy Pasha. More often, "legal" means have been utilized to eliminate opponents, as in the trials of military and civilian rivals in most Middle Eastern and many Black African states. In a number of these cases there were allegations of government pressure on the courts.

According to Z. K. Brzezinski, purges of power contenders by violence have been almost totally monopolized by totalitarian and authoritarian regimes. In his *The Permanent Purge*, Brzezinski argues that

> Totalitarianism needs the purge. *Disloyal and potential deviant individuals or groups must be unmasked and their followers liquidated. The tensions, conflicts and struggles within the totalitarian system must somehow be released or absorbed lest they disrupt into disintegrating violence. . . . The purposes of the purge are accordingly many and varied, and the need for it ever present.*[3]

It should be noted, however, that the same pressures as those described by Brzezinski have influenced the rash of purges that have appeared in Afro-Asia. In fact, in recent years the liquidation of opponents through the purge has diminished in Eastern Europe and even the chaos of the Chinese Cultural Revolution resulted only in the arrest and/or suicide of top leaders as physical violence was limited primarily to the military and revolutionary youth groups at lower levels. On the other hand, purges—that is, "trials" of "traitors" and "enemies of the people"—have increased in Afro-Asia, and particularly in Africa and the Middle East. In an era of increasing coups, the

---

[3] Brzezinski, 1956, p. 168. Italics in original.

Latin American practice of not executing the losers has not yet taken hold. Thus political opponents have been tried as traitors to the regime or state in the United Arab Republic, Sudan, Algeria, Morocco, Tanzania, Ghana, Libya, Sierra Leone, the Central African Republic, Syria, Iraq, Malawi, Ethiopia, Nigeria, the Ivory Coast, Niger, Iraq, Iran, Cameroon, both Congos, and Uganda, among others.

In defining establishment violence against power contenders, it appears useful to divide such acts between purges of elite opponents and large-scale conflict against sizable sections of the population involved in insurrection or civil war designed to overthrow the regime in power. In the interwar era those in power attempted to employ the force of the state to block major opposition in a series of bloody civil wars. The Bolsheviks successfully destroyed the power of the Whites and their foreign supporters. The Peking government abortively waged war against the Kuomintang forces in the 1920s, and the latter in turn attempted to deter the Communists in an on-again, off-again civil war that lasted two decades. Mexico experienced a series of efforts to overthrow the various regimes in power in Mexico City, and these efforts met with governmental responses of varying degrees of violence. In the West the most traumatic domestic strife was the unsuccessful Loyalist efforts to meet the challenge from the right in Spain. Other minor examples of establishment violence to meet insurrectionists took place in Latin America during this period.

In the postwar decades similar strife has developed on almost every continent as governments have attempted to deal with efforts to overthrow them. In Europe, Communist states have moved against unsuccessful insurrections in Hungary, Czechoslovakia, and East Germany. In the Western Hemisphere, violence was involved in establishment policies for meeting opposition in Cuba, Guatemala, Haiti, the Dominican Republic, Colombia, Bolivia, and Venezuela. In Africa similar activities were experienced in the Congo (Kinshasha), Uganda, Sudan, Rwanda, Yemen, Zanzibar, Cameroon, Morocco, and other polities, while in Asia almost every state has used the force of government to meet attempts to overthrow it. As Table 1–4 illustrates, coups and attempted coups with attendant violence have been a regular pattern in the developing world. Most of these attempted coups and revolts did not result in high-level political violence, although the numbers killed in Colombia, the Congo, Sudan, Bolivia, and Yemen were reportedly high. (Poor statistical information clouds the actual numbers, although the Yemen and Colombian cases, for example, were reported to be over 100,-000.)

The government's reply to attempted insurrection can be chillingly direct, taking the form of immediate execution of ringleaders and followers —perhaps with an added admonition similar to a Congolese warning that "all enemies of our people will perish in this way, miserably and lamentably"[4]—or it can be in "bureaucratese," as in the case of the order of the Hungarian Central Committee in the 1956 uprising declaring that it would be necessary

> to invoke a summary procedure throughout the country in order to punish acts aimed at the overthrow of the People's Republic, as well as acts of revolt, incitements to revolt, and conspiracy to the same end, assassination, murder, arson, the possession of explosives, . . . acts of violence against the authorities or individuals, illegal possession of arms. Persons found guilty under this summary procedure will be subject to the death penalty.[5]

There appears to be no simple pattern of government reaction to coup efforts. In many countries those in power have decided to "accept the inevitable" and have quietly retired from the field. This has been the normal procedure in Latin America and Southeast Asia, where an analysis of postwar coup efforts shows few killed or injured. Exceptions tend to be where military forces are divided in their loyalties and interservice rivalry has led to armed clashes causing military and civilian causalties, or where nonregular army units have attempted the overthrow of a regime. An example of the former was the navy-led coup in Thailand during the early 1950s that brought a violent reaction from the army and high causalties; the second type was exemplified by attempted coups in Haiti and the Dominican Republic.

Compared to other parts of the postwar world, Africa and the Middle East have experienced a greater number of bloody coups with deaths higher both during the event and in trials of opponents afterward. Perhaps the tradition of trying rivals has led to a greater willingness of the authorities to fight the insurrectionists and a stronger drive on the part of the winner to liquidate possible future opposition. If the alternatives provided in Latin America of exile or jail are not available to the loser, then violent resistance may appear more desirable.

EFFORTS TO INSTILL UNITY AND MAINTAIN ORDER

In its efforts to maintain order within the polity, the government may find it necessary to employ force against a variety of individuals and groups who seek to disrupt the system through protests against laws and policies, dramatizations of anti-government programs, burning or bombing institu-

[4] African Research Bulletin, April 1–30, 1970, p. 1729.

[5] Meray, 1969, p. 293.

tions considered friendly to the regime, assassinating officials, and so forth. These acts in themselves are designed to influence public decision-makers but are not part of an immediate plot to overthrow the establishment. When young American radicals bomb dozens of Bank of America buildings, when a group of Burmese students protest military policies, or when dissatisfied villagers in Thailand assassinate a hated local headman, they are not power contenders in the same sense as were Patrice Lumumba or Lavrenti Beria. Nevertheless, the establishment usually sees in them either a danger to orderly processes or the seeds of future revolt and seeks to halt their activities.

Government violence in these cases may take several forms, from police charges on demonstrations through regular court proceedings to quiet assassinations. In the West the police normally handle such cases, treating those who transgress the law for political purposes under the criminal code. Events in the United States, France, and Japan on occasion have reached such proportions as to necessitate the employment of larger paramilitary units. But even though regular police power was in these cases insufficient for the immediate quelling of the disturbances, the final dispositions of cases rising from the event will ultimately be decided by the courts.

Government reactions to similar events in the non-Western world often have involved initial countermeasures far more violent than those to be found in the West, where the killing of comparatively few students in the United States generated great furor. In Burma, China, India, and the Congo, for example, treatment of students and others confronting government forces has been speedy, pre-planned, and bloody. The numbers killed in clashes between the military and the Red Guards during the Chinese Cultural Revolution and in the riots in Indian cities probably have been considerably larger than those resulting from analogous confrontations in the West.

A second point to be noted about the maintenance of order in the developing states is that the courts either may not act after the authorities have used extensive violence to put down anti-government elements, or may actually employ extraordinary powers provided them by the establishment to punish the culprits. Show trials and public executions of political offenders have been used extensively in Afro-Asia during the past decade. Finally, we should take cognizance of the existence of so-called "black" groups— i.e., secret government enforcement units directed to punish without trial political deviants from lower levels of the political opposition. Although the most noted contemporary example of this technique is the semi-official Brazilian police liquidation of criminals, there is sufficient evidence that such "black" elements have been employed against political "criminals" in a number of developing nations.

Establishment violence against those employing "extra-legal" methods to confront the government is a constant cause for debate and litigation. In recent years differences of opinion on whether certain acts are actually crimes and whether those arrested could obtain a fair trial have reached even the relatively stable United States. The trials of the "Chicago Seven" and the Berrigans are examples of such disagreement.[6]

The second form of establishment violence involves force used against groups who desire political self-determination. This is not the place to enter into the full range of questions surrounding this issue. It is noteworthy, though, that while contemporary world opinion supports the right of colonial peoples to seek independence from metropolitan powers and the West generally favors the efforts of Soviet Jewry to emigrate to Israel and of East Germans to escape west, there is considerably less consensus on the right of self-determination of racial, ethnic, or cultural elements within the boundaries of states that have achieved sovereignty. Freedom for Indonesia, yes—Ambon, no! Independence for India and the Congo, yes—Hydrabad and Katanga, no! A sovereign Canada, of course—the liberation of Quebec, no!

Throughout Afro-Asia, governments have considered it necessary to employ force against secessionist elements who were prepared to fight for their political freedom; in the words of a Biafran rebel: "Give us Biafra or nothing. . . . Fourteen million Biafrans are under arms because we want to survive as a nation." [7] Wars of secession with various levels of violence have broken out in more than a dozen Afro-Asian states during the postwar period, the most violent of which have been in Indonesia (Ambon and parts of the outer islands), Pakistan (East Pakistani secession in 1971), Iran and Iraq (Kurdish nationalism), Burma (Shan, Chin Kachin, and Karen revolts that have lasted over twenty years), Congo (Kinshasha—Katanga and other tribal groups in the first years of independence), Ethiopia and Kenya (tribal units aided by outside forces), Chad (Northern Islamic Chieftaincies in a war in which the government has been aided by the French), Nigeria (Biafra), and China (Tibet).[8] Not even considered here are the Korean and Vietnamese wars that had aspects both of civil wars to establish a unified nation and of international conflict. In each of the cases listed above, the government decided to use armed force to maintain national unity, and in the majority of them the authorities have not been able to eliminate secessionist units completely.

[6] See the Walker Report in *Rights in Conflict*, 1968.

[7] *African Research Bulletin*, December 1–31, 1968, p. 1269.

[8] For a discussion of the issues involved in secession, see Anderson, von der Mehden, and Young, 1967, pp. 60–74.

Aside from these high-violence examples, there have been numerous other cases of individuals or groups practicing localized terrorism in situations not ripe for full-scale civil war. Even the West has not escaped this type of minor violence and the attendant forceful countermeasures of the government, as witnessed in the terror activities by French Canadian, Basque, Northern Irish, and Tyrolean secessionists. In the postwar era there have been no cases of peaceful and successful secession from sovereign states (not colonial empires), except in systems which could only be described as loose confederations. Thus, secession was achieved without violent counteraction from the central government only in Malaysia, where Singapore left soon after the formation of the central government, and in the weak unions of Egypt-Syria and Senegal-Mali. Other examples, such as the breakup of Ruanda-Urundi, French Equitorial and East Africa, and India and Pakistan, were part of the colonial settlement. New states have not been prepared to offer the same peaceful self-determination to dissatisfied sections of their populace that they desired from the colonial administrations. Instead they have replied with the sort of establishment violence that has been typical of national establishment reactions since time immemorial.

In some cases this type of establishment violence was formulated to instill unity within the polity rather than to contain separatist tendencies of primordial groups. Thus we have the "show trial" of "enemies of the state," which dramatizes the activities of political "criminals" in order to enlist the populace to support the government by or to bring about the psychological unification of those participating in the condemnation of those tried. Show trials intended to present the guilt of the opposition, often followed by the execution of the condemned, have been exploited in a number of Afro-Asian countries, most notably Syria, Congo, and both Vietnams. The example best known to Americans is the series of public trials in Cuba following Castro's victory. In those first months, hundreds were brought before mass meetings at which their "crimes" were exposed. The public became emotionally involved in the conviction, the "criminal" was executed, and the new regime was able to attract further support.

A more complex pattern was followed in Communist China during the early 1950s when the new government put an end to the moderate policies of the Korean War period. With the endorsement and urging of the regime, public clamor rose against landlords, merchants, and others who were accused of past and present crimes against the people. In this case, rather than selected large show trials of important personages, there were trials in villages and towns throughout the country of individuals accused of local crimes. In the process the entire village might meet to hear the indictment, give their own report of the crimes, and join in the judgment of the condemned. Numbers executed in these proceedings will probably never be known and calculations appear to differ depending upon the ideological tendencies of the reporter. Totals vary from tens of thousands to ten to twenty million.[9] Whatever the numbers, the trials aided the Communists to unify the nation after a bloody and long civil war. The involvement of the population helped to erase past enemies of the local citizenry, publish crimes of the former regime, and, perhaps most important, implicate the people as a whole in the "guilt" of liquidating friends of the Kuomintang at a time when there was still the possibility of a return to the mainland of the Nationalist forces with American backing.

QUELLING NONVIOLENT AND NONTHREATENING OPPOSITION

Although not as deadly as acts of governments against power contenders, secessionists, "undesirable" groups, and violent disruptors of public order, the use of violence against those presenting political views in a peaceful manner seems particularly reprehensible to Westerners.

To be sure, violence, as opposed to the mere threat of force, has not been used extensively to control peaceful expression, even in nondemocratic polities. In totalitarian and authoritarian systems the opposition either takes it for granted that the establishment will not accept diverse views and therefore seeks more direct means of attack, or it recognizes the limits of tolerance and attempts to work within them. When boundaries of allowed expression are crossed, the guilty are more likely to be jailed than executed (with obvious exceptions such as the policies of Hitler and Stalin).

In the postwar years, examples of arrest and conviction for "antigovernment" speech or writing have been extensive in Communist and authoritarian states, as illustrated by the treatment of writers in the Soviet Union and Yugoslavia and of newspaper editors in Taiwan, Greece, and Sukarno's Indonesia (where there was an unused death penalty for speaking against the president or his government). Of course, there have been occasions where violence was utilized in the arrest procedure and there have been cases where speaking against the state was part of a series of charges that resulted in execution.

There also have been occasions, in both authoritarian and democratic polities, when free public expression resulted in extensive deaths or injuries. Usually these have related to demonstrations, public gatherings, parades,

---

[9] Chou En-Lai reported that 830,000 "enemies of the people" were "destroyed," although Edgar Snow states that "destroyed" could be variously interpreted as "reduced," "dispersed," or "obliterated." For an unsympathetic analysis of these trials, see Walker, 1955.

picketing, and so forth. Violence normally has erupted when authorities have sought to control or disperse peaceful meetings or when extremists have attempted to escalate the gathering into confrontation with the establishment. Government action has been termed necessary because the meeting was technically illegal (lack of parade permit, injunction proceedings, or some such), the group had become disorderly, or, in nondemocratic countries, laws prohibit political meetings of any kind not sanctioned by the government. In the West examples of such confrontations have often involved students or, more recently, peace groups protesting the war in Vietnam. In Afro-Asia there have been heavier casualties as students and dissatisfied segments of the urban population have protested against the existence of the government itself.

In sum, this is a comparatively low-casualty form of establishment violence but one which results in high emotions.

ELIMINATION OF PERSONS OR GROUPS CONSIDERED "UNDESIRABLE"

One residual form of establishment violence has been singled out by world opinion as the most reprehensible. This is the form which is commonly called genocide, but which may extend beyond the liquidation of communal groups. In these cases the authorities judge it desirable or necessary to eliminate—not merely defeat, but eliminate—a particular group which, unlike power contenders, does not form an immediate danger to the establishment. Historic examples include the French massacre of the Protestants during the Reformation, bloodshed against Catholics by the followers of Martin Luther, Spanish treatment of Jews in the period of reconquest of the Peninsula, and Hitler's "final solution." In the postwar era charges of genocide have been made against government "repression" involving the Tutsi in Rwanda, Communists in Indonesia, Tibetans in Communist China, Ibo in Nigeria, southerners in Sudan, Indians in the Brazilian jungle, and blacks in the United States.

Many such allegations have been spurious, not in the sense that the events cited in the charges did not happen, but in the sense that they did not reflect a policy of genocide. For example, deaths may have resulted primarily from government policies designed to maintain order against separatist elements or against elements of minority groups attacking the establishment, or may have related to intercommunal friction in which the authorities were not directly involved. In fact, the heaviest casualties in this type of postwar event have been the intercommunal killings in Afro-Asia. Rarely in the days since the fall of Nazi Germany have there been blatant efforts by a government to "cleanse" the society of undesirable groups, the bulk of whom have not been conceived of as immediate dangers to the state. There have been cases, of course, where authorities have been indicted by sections of world opinion for moving in such a fashion as to cause needless deaths among "innocent" people involved in domestic conflicts. During the past decade the two most notable examples of this charge have been against the Nigerian and Pakistani governments, both of whom were accused of not moving with sufficient speed to care for defeated rivals and of not allowing foreign relief aid into war-damaged regions with enough alacrity to prevent mass deaths from starvation and disease.

Although no government in the postwar years can be clearly indicted for outright domestic "genocide," there have been several cases in which large sections of a population have been eliminated with at least tacit approval of the government in power. Among the most prominent cases have been those involving Rwanda, Cambodia, Tibet, Sudan, and Indonesia. Several of these examples will be analyzed in detail in the next chapter.

ESTABLISHMENT JUSTIFICATIONS OF VIOLENCE   It is striking that the rationales employed by establishments or power holders for their acts of violence against opponents are similar to those articulated by anti-establishment spokesmen. In brief compass we might note the following kinds of justifications.

DEFENSE

Just as anti-government forces have argued the necessity of employing violence to protect themselves from measures employed by the authorities, so the ruling elite has voiced the need to defend itself and its people. Three types of defense justifications commonly are presented. First, force has been declared to be required against those seeking to destroy the state through revolution or secession. In these circumstances force is termed legitimate as the only means to maintain the integrity of the state. When rivals are accused of working with external powers, violence takes on even more legitimacy. Second, in the highly personal regimes of Afro-Asia, violent reactions have been "compelled" by the need to protect the leader and his colleagues. In these cases the rhetoric has stressed less the defense of the state and more the attacks on "the leader" such as Premier Nkrumah, the Shah of Iran, the King of Morocco, President Sukarno, or King Hussein of Jordan. At times the elite group itself may define the need for collective self-defense, as did the Indonesian leadership following the attempted coup of 1965. At that time the military insisted that, "If we hadn't killed them, they would have killed us." [10] Normally, government justifications are less stark.

[10] Brackman, 1969, p. 189. General Nasution declared that the Communists were planning other killings; this charge was repeated by President Suharto and other military leaders.

Finally, violence is defended as necessary to maintain public order against political opponents described as dangerous to the lives and property of the citizens of the state. Police power is required as a normal function of the state in protecting its population from the activities of those who employ violent disruption, political kidnappings, arson, and murder.

Force used to quiet free expression is declared to be necessary in order to defend the state from statements that could foster disunity or treason, and even genocide has been supported as cutting out "cancerous growths" from the body politic.

CHARACTER OF THE OPPOSITION

Many governments have sought to justify violence in terms of the character of the opposition, which is described as having unpopular, treasonous, dangerous, or weak qualities. When utilizing force against rivals, disruptors, secessionists, or "undesirables," governments have publicized these claims to diminish opponents' popularity, to camouflage real reasons for action, to bring policies into line with ideology, to build support for the regime, or, in some cases, to accurately describe the opposition. Among the specific allegations encountered are these:

1. Bogus Leadership–Bogus Opposition   The leadership of the opposition did not reflect the true will of those it was representing. This argument has been used most often in secessionist situations and repeats almost word for word the charges leveled against nationalists by colonial powers. In fact, during the United Nations debates over Indonesian independence, the Dutch delegate used a speech the Indian representative had used to defend her country's takeover of separatist-minded Hyderabad, exchanging the words India for Holland and Hyderabad for Indonesia. Force against separatists in Indonesia, the Congo, China, and Burma, for example, has been legitimized on the alleged ground that the government was representing the real desires of the region against their leaders.

2. Foreign Interference   Force is acceptable because government opponents are being aided by foreign powers. The two foreign agencies most often accused of interference in domestic affairs are the Communists (particularly the Chinese) and the American Central Intelligence Agency. However, alleged international interlopers also have included neighboring nations, as exemplified by charges of Egyptian activities throughout the Middle East, the execution of "traitors" in the same region for working for "International Zionism," Somali aid to tribal groups in Kenya and Ethiopia, Indonesian support of rebels in Malaysia, Indian arming and training of East Pakistani secessionists, and Cuban backing of revolutionaries throughout Latin America. A rather typical statement justifying action against those who worked with such foreign powers was made by the Sudanese government when putting down a coup:

> It was clear this group had been exploited by the forces of reactionary sedition and were conspiring to execute its aim of transforming Wad Nubawi into a bloody field and staging post of a bloody plan hatched by international imperialists and reactionary forces.[11]

                          3. Inimical Domestic Interests   Developing nations in particular have described the opposition as representing domestic interests inimical to the interests of the population. Thus in Tibet the Chinese Communists justified actions against the revolt in the early sixties on the grounds that it was fomented by reactionary feudal and theocratic forces that had long subjugated the people; in Indonesia revolts in the outer islands in the 1950s were described by the Sukarno government as being led by feudal elements; and in Burma Shan rebels were described by the Rangoon government as being duped by traditional leaders attempting to protect themselves and the opium traffic.

                          4. Immorality   Responding to the opposition's claims that the government and its policies were immoral, the establishment has attacked its critics as maintaining questionable values, using terror tactics that rejected the importance of human life, living improper life styles, and generally setting themselves against the moral standards of the community. Those attacked as thus inferior or "undesirable" became more vulnerable to government programs directed against them.

VENGEANCE

Violence has been termed legitimate as vengeance against terror activities of the opposition. This demand for retribution has led to heavy casualties, particularly in guerrilla wars, or when members of the government or military have seen their own killed. In Indonesia the military justified the liquidation of the Communists in 1965, at least in part, because of the alleged

---

11 *African Research Bulletin*, March 1–31, 1970, p. 1705. An army leader at the time of the attempted Indonesian coup condemned the perpetrators of the action, declaring, "Since they have committed treason, they must be destroyed and quarantined from all activities in the fatherland." Brackman, 1969, p. 193.

cruel assassination of several high officers in the first hours of the attempted coup. Some French officers in Algeria and both sides in the Vietnam war have claimed atrocities by the enemy as reasons for violent reaction.

NECESSITY

Violence has been described as necessary when anti-establishment forces refuse to accept peaceful negotiation or accommodation. Just as the opposition legitimized force on the grounds of governmental intransigence, so the authorities have described their opponents as extremists in their demands, anarchists or nihilists in their tactics and philosophy, and ideologically opposed to peaceful solutions. Most Western governments have argued that violence by national or local authorities against their own citizens was used only when a situation developed which endangered life or property and peaceful persuasion had failed. Thus, the use or nonuse of various weapons has depended upon the specific situation and was justified as necessary for the maintenance of law and order.

DEVELOPMENT OF UNITY

There have been cases where government leadership has argued that some forms of violence are necessary to establish national unity. Trials of "bad" landlords, "criminal" former leaders, economic "parasites," or other "traitors" of the people were considered useful in developing support for the regime and cleaning out dangerous elements. However, few would go as far as Stalin when he recommended that, "from time to time, the master must without fail go through the ranks of the Party with a broom in his hands," [12] particularly when that "broom" proved to be purge trials.

In sum, every nation has found it necessary to use force to combat those who perpetrate crimes against the community. The vast majority of these cases of violent coercion have received the support of the society, regardless of their political persuasion. Establishment violence has divided the community when it has been perceived as directed in an unequal manner toward a particular section of the polity through a biased use of ordinary criminal law or through the force of the regime directed against political opponents. The former tends to be found more often in polities with primordial minorities who either have been maintained in subservient positions through law, as the Chinese in several Southeast Asian states and

[12] Brzezinski, 1956, p. 38.

the blacks in South Africa (a political "minority"), or have been perceived to be deprived of equal protection of the laws.

The partisan use of violence has been largely absent from Western Europe and North America, except in rare instances when there have been attempts to overthrow regimes or when secessionist elements have arisen. In these regions the employment of force by the authorities in political situations normally has been related to the maintenance of "law and order" in political demonstrations. In the developing world, on the other hand, establishment violence involving coups, revolutions, and communal strife has been experienced in the vast majority of countries. Wherever it has happened the justifications for its utilization often have been the other side of the coin of anti-establishment legitimizations of violence.

SELECT CAUSES OF POLITICAL VIOLENCE part two

The single most important feature of Zanzibar's contemporary political development has been the failure of nationalism to unify the population. . . . Class boundaries did not usually cut across racial boundaries but coincided with them.

M. Lofchie (1965, pp. 69 and 83)

THE CLASS-COMMUNAL PATTERN

4

The basic idea of this chapter is that high levels of political violence will tend to be precipitated by a coincidence of class and communal antagonisms. It is the rare case when large-scale domestic conflict can be laid at the door of only one cause. But among causal situations, one of the most volatile would appear to be the *perception* of a communal group that it is being economically or socially subjugated by another primordially based class. The word "perceived" is emphasized because it is the contention here that there need be no objective economic or social difference so long as the politically active element of the lower class perceives, or chooses to perceive, that it is being kept in an inferior position. In either case, whether subjective or objective, when class inequality is paralled by communal separation, the end result tends to be a situation of heightened tensions. When a catalytic event such as a coup, a foreign intervention, the assassination of a communal leader, or the achievement of independence is interjected, this combination of antagonisms has led to some of the most bloody instances of postwar internal violence.

"Class" as discussed here is not considered in its Marxian connotation. In communal-class divisions, often the rhetoric and perceptions of the group that considers itself subjugated join together elements that traditional Marxist theory would term mutually antagonistic. This uniting of disparate economic classes against a common foe has been recognized by nationalist writers who have commented upon the different class balance established by imperialism. For example, the interwar Indonesian Islamic nationalist, Harsono Tjokroaminoto, once argued with indigenous Communists that the clash with the Dutch government was class war—the Dutch, Christian capitalists against the Indonesian, Moslem downtrodden native.[1] Although

---

[1] For an analysis of this attitude see von der Mehden, 1963, pp. 58–61.

Communists rejected this formulation, we must remark that communal conflict has allowed competing economic "classes," in the traditional sense, to overlook differences within the group.

Several examples of class-communal violence will be discussed to illustrate this pattern. These include the Cambodian killing of Vietnamese in 1970–71, the Indonesian "massacre" of Communists in 1965–66, the Tutsi-Hutu conflict in Rwanda in 1963, the Zanzibar "Revolution" of 1964, and the massacre of Ibo in Northern Nigeria in 1966. On a smaller scale we will consider primarily intercommunal confrontations like the Malay-Chinese riots in Malaysia in 1969, Catholic-Protestant violence in Northern Ireland since 1969, and black-white conflicts in the United States in the 1960s. In total deaths these cases ranged from less than a thousand for all of the last three examples to tens to hundreds of thousands in most of the others.

CAMBODIA, 1970–71

In early 1970 the political situation in Cambodia had become highly unstable as the result of domestic economic and political problems and foreign pressure. While the long-time Premier, Prince Sihanouk, visited abroad, a coalition of military and civilian leaders staged a coup which at the time was largely bloodless but which was followed by a series of violent events. These resulted from the revitalization of the old left-wing opposition, the government-supported Vietnamese and American incursion into the country to root out Communist sanctuaries and support the shaky new regime, and increased military activity by North Vietnamese and National Liberation Front units.

When the new government came into power, reports began to filter in from rural areas of massacres of members of the Vietnamese minority by the Cambodian populace.[2] Apparently these executions were the work of both local Khmer (Cambodian) villagers and elements of the ill-organized army. The government initially did little to stop these killings and at one point even launched an official propaganda campaign against the indigenous Vietnamese, reminding the populace of past Khmer victories over their ancient rivals. Apparently this propaganda was designed to increase support for the new regime and may have been motivated by the government's fear of the allegedly pro-NLF sympathies of the Vietnamese. The exact number killed will probably never be known, but large numbers of bodies were seen by foreign observers. The Cambodian Foreign Minister admitted to 3,500 deaths in a one-month period and there were unconfirmed reports that over 200,000 were killed. Without doubt massacres of civilians did take place and casualties were heavy.

2 *New York Times* and *Facts on File*, April 1970.

The Vietnamese fit the pattern of a pariah community, just as the Chinese do in Southeast Asia, but in this case emotions against the Vietnamese ran particularly high in rural regions. Historically, there had been considerable conflict between the Cambodians and what is now Vietnam, with peace coming only with French rule over both. During the French period Vietnamese held important positions in the civil service, urban economy, and agriculture.[3] In urban centers they included some rich merchants and former high government servants, but most were technicians, lesser merchants, mechanics, nongovernment office clerks, and artisans. In rural areas they took over some of the best land in eastern and southern Cambodia. Industrious, aggressive, and efficient farmers and fishermen, they were met with antipathy from the indigenous population, who preferred moving away to working beside the "invaders."

The Vietnamese also maintained themselves separately from the majority community. They dressed distinctively, generally could not speak Cambodian fluently, and included a high percentage of Christians in a Buddhist country.

It is interesting to note the different attitude held toward the Chinese community, which dominated the apex of the economic pyramid in Cambodia as in so many other Southeast Asian countries. Like the Vietnamese, the Chinese too were victims of persecution, but on a much smaller scale. This was in part because of the rural nature of much of the violence and in part because Cambodian attitudes toward the Chinese were more ambivalent. Envied for their wealth, the Chinese have been admired for their industriousness and shrewdness. They have intermarried with the Cambodians who allegedly prize their lighter skin. According to one observer, "In Khmer eyes, the Chinese male is a superb breadwinner, and many Cambodian fathers dream of a Chinese son-in-law."[4] In addition, the Chinese have not been ancient enemies of the Cambodians, as the Vietnamese have.

In sum, the Vietnamese in Cambodia formed a distinct communal group who were perceived to have undesirable personal characteristics and who held economic positions that put them in direct conflict with the Cambodian population. As skilled workers and richer rice farmers they were in direct competition with the Cambodians. In rural areas, where the greatest violence was precipitated, they were considered interlopers who held the better land. Class divisions thus exacerbated traditional antipathies between the communities.

[3] For a discussion of the role of the Vietnamese in Cambodia see, Steinberg et al., 1957; Williams, 1970; Zadrozny, 1955; and Willmott, 1967.

[4] Steinberg, 1957, p. 47. For an excellent discussion of differing attitudes toward Chinese and Vietnamese, see Willmott, 1967.

INDONESIA, 1965–66

On the night of September 30, 1965, a group of disgruntled officers kidnapped and killed several high Indonesian military officers in an effort that has variously been described as an unsuccessful military coup, an abortive Communist coup, and an attempt to forestall a coup by other elements of the military. Whatever it was, it collapsed and the defeated officers involved were killed in action or executed. Although the attempt was short-lived, the aftermath was extremely violent because of the murder of the Indonesian generals and the alleged complicity of the Communists. To the present day there is intense debate as to the exact role of the Indonesian Communist Party (PKI) in the planning and implementation of the coup. Most experts now agree that party leaders played some role in the events, although just what role is not clear.[5] Be that as it may, the event enabled both the civilian and military rivals of the PKI to destroy the organization and large sections of its membership.

In the ensuing months, party leaders, members, suspected members, and in some cases their families were killed. The first deaths came from military operations planned to eliminate Communist leadership and strong points. Most of these initial killings, resulting from confrontations between the military and ill-armed PKI units and their allies, were apparently in West and Central Java. What followed, however, were mass and individual executions by villagers, Moslem youth groups, and other noncentral government units, particularly in East Java, Bali, and the outer islands of the Republic. Here the military apparently offered its blessings to vigilante-type activities which had as their targets both local Communists and, in some cases, nonparty rivals.[6] In time the pariah Chinese community also came under attack, but it would be inaccurate to describe these activities as directed primarily against the Chinese. Ultimately, in a few short months in late 1965 and early 1966, probably 200,000 to 400,000 were killed, 35,000 to 100,000 in East Java alone.[7] The exact number will never be known.

Of particular interest here are the killings at the local level and especially those in rural Java. This too has been a matter of speculation and debate, so that what follows must be considered as only part of the story until further research is accomplished.

In the months following the attempted coup individuals were killed in rural Java for a host of reasons; probably a large number of these deaths resulted from apolitical personal grudges. The deaths of many PKI members,

---

[5] For a discussion of different views on the role of the PKI, see Bass, 1970.

[6] See Hughes, 1967; Brackman, 1969; and Vittachi, 1967.

[7] For a good discussion of the possible numbers killed and of the public reporting of the event, see Brackman, 1969, pp. 120–26, and Hughes, 1967, pp. 184–89.

however, appears to have had some basis in the communal-class relationships of East and Central Java, although evidence for this conclusion is only suppositional.

Javanese rural society is usually divided into three culturo-religious elements, the *prijajis* (aristocratic-traditional), the *abangan* (poorer-traditional), and the *santris* (most devout Moslems). The *abangan* tend to be more secularist and nominal in their obeisance to Islam and poorer economically. The *santris*, who tend to be made up of the middle economic strata of shopkeepers, small landowners, and managers of small industries, have given their religious and political loyalty to Islam. As Ruth McVey has pointed out,

> *This cultural schism [between the* abangan *and the* santris*] grew wider as it became identified with political organization, so that the political and cultural antagonisms have tended to reinforce each other. Also, there has been an identification of Islam with rural wealth, . . . whereas the Communists have put themselves as sponsors of the poor.*[8]

Thus it was natural that the PKI would appeal to the *abangan* and exploit their fears of and dislike for the *santri*. The *santris* for their part became the backbone of the Islamic parties and the *santri-abangan* schism had become one of the important facts of political life at both the local and national levels. In an early Communist rebellion in 1948, *santri* elements opposed the PKI and the national elections of the mid-1950s gave further evidence of this split.

One further element was injected into this tense situation. In 1960 the government instituted a land reform bill which set limits on landholdings. Even if the program were successful, the already high population and comparatively small size of land plots meant that the land reforms would only have provided some 500,000 acres to Java's poor and landless. However, because of inflation, maladministration, and political pressure, only 1,500 hectares were distributed by February 1963.[9] Thus, in 1964 the PKI vocally attacked landlords who refused to abide by the land law and initiated a program called "one-sided actions." This policy called for the em-

---

[8] McVey, 1970, p. 7. The *abangan-santri-priaji* concept was most fully discussed by Clifford Geertz. See, for example, his excellent *The Religion of Java*, 1960.

[9] See Hindley, 1964, pp. 1–17 and 176–77. The exact class nature of this conflict has been a topic of considerable discussion with the most vigorous position being taken by W. Wertheim in his papers and articles; see Wertheim, 1966. In these statements he argues that land issues were also part of the cause of massacres in Christian and Hindu areas, stating that on Timor killings were led by Catholic leaders and landlords.

ployment of extralegal means by the Communists to force obedience to the law, which in turn generated further tensions between elements of the *abangan* and the *santri,* for the latter tended to be the landholders affected by the reform.

When the abortive coup took place, emotions already ran high on both a communal and class basis, with religious groups seeing the Communists not only as secular rivals to their political power and ideological antagonists, but also as the instigators of policies designed to weaken their economic position. In East and Central Java the massacres themselves were in part perpetrated by Moslem youth organization members and, some would argue, by landowners from the *santri*-based Moslem political organizations. Certainly culturo-religious and economic tensions were exacerbated by the land issue and were factors in the island's violence.

RWANDA,
1963–64

Rwanda is a small, comparatively heavily populated nation in Central Africa, formerly part of the Belgian colony of Ruanda-Urundi. Even prior to the attainment of independence in 1962 there had been violence between the majority Hutu ethnic group (83 percent) and the ruling Tutsi (less than 15 percent). In 1959 Tutsi extremists attempted to assassinate Hutu leaders, resulting in violent reactions from the Hutu populace. A year later national elections brought an overwhelming victory to the Hutu political organization, *Parmehutu,* resulting in further conflict. Many Tutsi fled in panic to neighboring Burundi. Tensions became even higher when Tutsi refugees formed a paramilitary organization called the *Inyenzi* (cockroaches) and attacked back into Rwanda.[10]

There were still some 250,000 Tutsi residing in the country when the invasion came in 1963. The entrance of armed Inyenzi appeared to cause mass hysteria among the Hutu. At the national level Tutsi delegates, party members, and ministers were arrested and executed without trial. In order to "protect the country" ministers were put in charge of each of the ten prefectures and given control over local authorities and elected headmen. In the rural areas the populace ran amok—apparently with support from local leaders. The massacres of Tutsis reportedly brought death to some 10,000 to 15,000, although the government claimed that only 750 were killed, including 400 civilians. Attacks by Inyenzi continued into the next year, as did arrests and reprisals. Ultimately, there were 150,000 Tutsi refugees in Burundi, Uganda, the Congo, and Tanzania while the remaining 120,000 were not allowed to leave because of fears that they would join the Inyenzi.

[10] For discussions of these events see African Centre, n.d.; Segal, 1964; and Lemarchand, 1970.

Traditional feudalism was the primary source of much of the conflict that developed in Rwanda.[11] Through several centuries a rigid class system had been established in which the majority became dominated by the Tutsi. Under this feudal pattern contractual relations existed through which those in inferior positions offered their services to someone with higher prestige or more cattle in turn for protection. Both Hutu and Tutsi were held within this contractual relationship, but the Hutu were obviously on the bottom of the economic, social, and political system until the events of the 1960s. Differentiations existed between the two ethnic groups on several bases:

1. The most obvious difference was physical; the stereotype of the Tutsi was tall, thin, and austere, while the Hutu tended to be small and heavier.[12]

2. The Tutsi controlled the cattle, the major source of wealth, and the client system made it possible for the better off among them to live without doing menial work. The Hutu were basically the land tillers and the Tutsi the cattle raisers.

3. The Tutsi controlled the civil service and under the Belgians were able to dominate the political structure until 1960. Until quite late in Belgian rule this control was aided both by traditional advantages and by modern educational opportunities available to the minority group.[13]

4. Finally, the years of feudalism had helped to establish a psychological pat- of inferior-superior relationships between the two peoples.[14]

The result of this system was a feudal communal-class schism extremely rare in the modern world—one in which, according to a Pastoral Letter of Monsignor Peraudin prepared in 1959,

> social differences and inequalities are to a large extent tied to racial differences, in this sense, that wealth on the one hand and political and even judicial power on the other are, in reality, in considerable proportion in the hands of people of one race.[15]

This traditional pattern could not outlast democratic elections or independence without extreme stress, shattering it finally through massacre and emigration.

[11] For a thorough analysis of the feudal system see Lemarchand, 1970, and Maquet, 1961.

[12] Maquet, 1961, p. 145.

[13] Lemarchand, 1970, pp. 134–36.

[14] Segal, 1964, p. 11.

[15] African Centre, n.d., p. 2.

ZANZIBAR,
1964

In early 1964 Africans (Shirazis) from the island of Zanzibar and from the mainland rose against the Arab-controlled regime in a revolt that resulted in the establishment of a "Revolutionary" government and ultimately in union with Tanganyika to form Tanzania. Deaths from the event totaled some two to three thousand, mostly Arabs, who were killed either by the victorious revolutionary forces, in what a *New York Times* correspondent termed "political liquidation," or through mob action by the African population. The coup itself was swift and the fighting short-lived, but thousands of Arabs and Asians were interned, and in the ensuing year large-scale emigration left only one tenth of the Arab and one third of the Asian communities on the island. Low-level violence continued for several years.[16]

Communal-class tensions had been developing over a long period and had erupted into violent rioting four times previously. It was almost a classic situation. During the colonial period the population was composed of four major elements, the Arabs who made up almost 17 percent, the Shirazis and mainland Africans who were the vast majority with somewhat over 75 percent, and a residual collection of various nationalities, primarily Indian, Pakistani, and European. The primary conflict was between the Shirazi-African populace and the Arabs and, to a lesser extent, the Asians. The sources of this tension could be traced back to historic, social, economic, and political divisions which split the island.

Historically, the Arabs had long dominated the clove and coconut plantations upon which the island depended for its export earnings. They also had been deeply involved in earlier slave trade, which left bitter memories in African minds. Black nationalists and their newspaper outlets printed detailed accounts of past Arab cruelties toward their ancestors. These stories increased in the years prior to the revolt and helped to deepen emotions.

Socially as well the Shirazi-African citizenry saw themselves as underprivileged. Education was dominated by the Asians and Arabs, so that only a very small segment of the majority population was technically equipped for professional positions. Education at the higher levels was the dominion of the Arabs and Asians, as only 11 percent of Standards VII–IX (middle school) and 2.9 percent of Standards X–XII (upper school) were Shirazi. One observer has noted that insufficient intermarriage and social or economic mobility also have tended to separate the people. In addition, the

[16] For a chronology of events see the *African Research Bulletin* and the *New York Times*, January-February 1964.

static nature of the island's agricultural economy also severely limited the upward mobility of Africans.[17]

Most observers appear to agree that the economic issues dividing the two communities were of prime importance in leading the nation to violence. Here perceptions were as important as reality as the bulk of the Arab population was not significantly different in economic position from the majority communal elements, although they kept their Arab identities for cultural reasons and cooperated with the Arab elite. The upper- and middle-class Arabs epitomized the Arabs to the Shirazis and Africans, however. In the all-important plantation industry, no African or Shirazi owned a single piece of land with over three thousand trees, more than two-thirds of such plantations being held by Arabs and the rest by Asians. This large landholding monopoly grew particularly important as Shirazi moved into rural areas in the middle of the twentieth century and came into conflict with Arab landlords and into contact with the bitterly anti-Arab African plantation workers. In the urban areas the Arabs and Asians also controlled the economy. One study of the urban class structure showed the upper class to be 95 percent Arab-Asian with no one from the majority group, the upper-middle class 21 percent Arab and 49 percent Asian, and the nonmenial middle class 25 percent Arab and 32 percent Asian.[18]

This near monopoly of education and of the economy led to political power in the colonial period as the Arabs in particular came to dominate the civil service. The Arabs and Asians fought for communal representation, fearing that "one-man one-vote" would decrease their power. Even during this time communal problems dominated politics, particularly issues involving land ownership and squatters' rights. When independence arrived in 1963, it was only a matter of time before this situation would be tested and the majority would demand not only its full political rights but a greater control of the social and economic structure as well. When the time came in 1964, the former elite was almost completely ousted.

Zanzibar thus had all the elements of the class-communal pattern. A majority communal group perceived itself as deprived of its economic, social, and political rights by another primordial class and, most importantly, "Class boundaries did not usually cut across racial boundaries but coincided with them."[19]

---

[17] Lofchie, 1965, pp. 93–94. This is an excellent background study on the sociocultural differences on the island. Also see Herrick, et al., 1968. Religion did not form a basis for division inasmuch as over 90 percent of the people were Moslem.

[18] Lofchie, 1965, p. 89.

[19] *Ibid.*, p. 83.

NORTHERN NIGERIA, 1966

The Biafra secessionist movement held world attention for three years and received considerable reportage, some of it highly emotional in tone. An understanding of that conflict and of the central idea of this chapter can be gained by analyzing the massacres of the Ibo in Northern Nigeria in 1966. Violence against the Ibo originally developed in May 1966 when local students, politicians, bureaucrats, and businessmen led attacks on Ibo communities first in Kano, then in Zaria, Kaduna, and other towns. This was a period when the nation was controlled by an allegedly pro-Ibo military clique charged with the killing of leaders of the Northern region, where strong secessionist and anti-Ibo sentiments were manifest. Another military coup in July, this time against the so-called "Ibo Coup," was the catalyst that sparked a general massacre led by the same elements as in the May pogrom, with the addition of some military units. Between 10,000 and 30,000 Ibos were killed and the rest fled to their homelands in the southeast.[20] These massacres were to set the stage for the secession of Biafra.

Antagonisms between the Ibo and the Hausa-Fulani majority in the North were similar in character to those we have seen in Cambodia and Zanzibar. Under the British, Northern Nigeria had been "protected" from the inroads of missionaries and Western education while the Ibo had taken advantage of modern training.[21] As a result, major differences were produced between the two communities. The Northerners remained Moslem while the Ibo developed Christian leadership. Educational disparities appear to have been a key to tensions in the area. In 1947 only 2.5 percent of those receiving a secondary education were Northerners and in 1951 there was only one full university graduate from the region and he was a converted Christian. At the time of independence, less than 10 percent of those attending school in the new nation were from the North, despite the fact that the region held a majority of the population.[22] This educational headstart of the Ibo, when combined with a certain aggressiveness in their character and the traditional values of the Hausa-Fulani, established Southerners living in the North as a special class. In the national civil service it was difficult to obtain qualified Northerners, so that as of 1961 they held less than 1 percent of the top posts. The minority also dominated

[20] For a discussion of these events, see Schwarz, 1968, and Nwankwo and Ifejika, 1969.

[21] For an analysis of the colonial period see Coleman, 1958.

[22] Schwarz, 1968, pp. 47–49; Nwankwo and Ifejika, 1969, pp. 27–28; and Sklar and Whitaker, 1966, pp. 25–26.

the skilled, technological, and office positions, as well as trade. The Northerners also found themselves competing with better educated opponents in the political field. As of 1957 there were no university graduates in either Northern regional legislative body and at the national level their percentage of representatives with a university education was only a quarter that of the Southerners. The populace recognized this inequality; during the 1966 riots the fingers of Ibo students were cut off, in the hope of curtailing "the educational lead of Eastern Nigeria over the North." [23]

The communal groups were further segregated by language, dress, and residence. Few Northerners had been taught English by the British during the colonial period and even the dress of the two communities was distinctive as Ibo civil servants often mirrored their former rulers. Ibos living in Northern cities maintained themselves in communal ghettos which became targets of arson and looting during the pogroms. Even the universities became tribalized.

Thus tensions were created in the region by the injection of a foreign community with better education in the modern sense, a different culture and religion, an aggressive character, and greater economic power. These were qualities the British had as well, but they had military power. After July 1966 the Ibo in the North were without protection.

In the three cases that follow, the level of violence, in terms of the number of deaths, has been relatively low and casualties have come primarily from efforts of authorities to maintain order in intercommunal conflicts. It should be noted, however, that in each case the police or military have been accused of favoritism.

NORTHERN IRELAND, 1969– The complaints of the Catholics of Northern Ireland have a number of similarities with those of blacks in the United States, although the histories of the two people have been quite different. In fact, one pro-Catholic writer, although aware that he was oversimplifying the matter, declared that "In Northern Ireland Catholics are Blacks who happen to have white skins." [24] Even some of the symbols and rhetoric are the same, as the Catholics have adopted the song "We Shall Overcome" and recently have begun to call their crusade one of "Civil Rights." (Although the term was used in Northern Ireland as early as the 1930s, its prominent

23 Schwarz, 1968, p. 217.
24 De Paar, 1970, p. 13.

reemergence now clearly is connected with the black civil rights movement in America.)

Violence has been no stranger to this section of the island, and no effort will be made here to describe the centuries of conflict that have troubled the Six Countries.[25] The most recent upsurge of violence dates from 1969 when the Catholics renewed their efforts to wrest what they considered to be their rights from the dominant Protestant majority. Deaths and injuries have resulted from confrontations of the two communal groups with Northern Irish and British authorities in demonstrations, riots, arson, sniping, and fire fights. Yet for all the smoke, rhetoric, and riots, deaths have been comparatively low when compared to the five previously described cases. During the first half of tension-ridden 1971 less than thirty persons were reported as killed and during the first three years of conflict fewer than 400 lost their lives.

Filtering out the reasons for the dispute is difficult in situations of this sort, where descriptions are often highly biased and emotional in content. The communal differences would appear to be obvious between the majority Protestants and the Catholics, who have composed some 33–34 percent of the population for the past sixty years. The Protestants appear to consider Roman Catholicism to be the paramount issue and have been particularly disturbed by the possible influence of the Church on its adherents, by religious rules on the education of children of mixed marriages, and by the potential danger of ties with Catholic Eire. The activities of the outlawed Irish Republican Army (IRA), court decisions appearing to support the Catholic position in Eire, and parades celebrating victories of the past have not helped. However, most outside observers and spokesmen for the Catholics have disputed the argument that religion and Irish unity are the prime bases of the present conflict, pointing to social and economic disparities between the two groups. As the fiery Bernadette Devlin wrote in 1969, "What we must at all times make clear is that we are fighting for the economic rights of an underprivileged people, not to win back the Six Countries for Ireland."[26] These complaints again have points in common with those of Blacks in the United States:

1. Economic   Catholics have accused the majority of keeping them in lower economic positions. They note that their unemployment rate has run twice as high as that of the Protestants and that this rate has run far ahead of the percentage for the rest of the United

---

[25] For a history of events in earlier years see Boyd, 1969. It is very difficult to find objective studies of these events.

[26] Devlin, 1969, p. 167.

Kingdom. It is charged that small Protestant-owned industries do not employ Catholics, that there are no Catholics in higher positions in large firms, and that they have been frozen out of skilled unions where jobs are passed down from father to son. These charges were largely true in the past, although, as in the United States, things have been changing. Those around Miss Devlin have described themselves as socialists and have attempted to make common cause with Protestant workers against the gentry and industrialists, but to little avail.

2. *Social*   Northern Ireland has segregated education and housing. Primary and secondary schools are almost entirely segregated, although the students are brought together at the university level (except for teaching colleges). Unlike the United States, segregation in Ireland long has been the desire of large segments of both populations, for the Catholic schools offer different religious training and the teaching of the Irish language and Irish history. Housing segregation has been de facto and, it is charged, de jure. There tend to be Catholic and Protestant sections in the cities and the former have accused Protestant-dominated city governments of favoritism in public housing.[27] The dangers to those families living in communities of a different faith have been readily apparent at the time of riots when they have been the targets of communal antagonisms.

3. *Political*   Party affiliation has also divided the two communities as Protestants normally have supported the Unionists and Catholics the Nationalists. The minority has complained of gerrymandering, dictatorial powers implemented by the central government, and biased legislation and administration by local authorities. For example, one Catholic stated that in a county where those of his faith composed 53 percent of the population they held only 32 county positions versus 338 held by Protestants.[28] A key issue in local and national politics has been the role of the police, who have been accused of anti-Catholic bias. Emotions have risen so high in this matter that Miss Devlin once counseled that if she had her way she would give the police three weeks, "for every honest man to get out of it, then systematically shoot the rest." [29]

Thus, in the Northern Irish case as in those examined earlier, perceived economic, social, and political differences divided two primordial

[27] De Paar, 1970, p. 155.

[28] *Ibid.* For other versions of events and issues see Wallace, 1970, and Riddell, 1970.

[29] Devlin, 1969, p. 149.

groups into communal-class antagonists. The unwillingness of the Protestant government and of the British to employ the kind of counter-force used in places such as Rwanda, Pakistan, and Indonesia must, at least in part, be the explanation for the low level of casualties.

MALAYSIA, 1969 Foreign and local observers have long reported Malaysia to be on the brink of serious communal warfare. Through the first dozen years of independence the nation experienced several low- or medium-level communal riots involving Malay and Chinese elements.[30] These incidents were most serious in 1964, 1965, and 1967, with casualties primarily resulting from clashes between Chinese supporters of the Socialist Front party and Malay authorities. However, until 1969 the government prided itself on the relative peace in Peninsula Malay (now Western Malaysia). It was thus a shock to the political system when large-scale rioting, looting, arson, and confrontations with authorities broke out in May 1969. The catalyst was the national elections which had raised emotions and brought a reduced margin of victory to the ruling Alliance Party. Casualties totaling 196 dead and 439 wounded resulted from intercommunal clashes and confrontations with the authorities as they sought to bring order. (The unofficial death count was 300 to 700.) Although this violence, which lasted more than two months, was a severe blow to Malaysian official optimism, the situation in fact was such that it well might have provided the basis for even higher casualties.

Communal violence has been an integral part of Malayan history, with the Chinese and Malays both victims and perpetrators. External forces often have been involved in these events. The Japanese occupation and its aftermath brought attacks on the Chinese community while the attempts of the Communist Party to overthrow the colonial government in the "Emergency" of 1948–60 were primarily a Chinese project.[31] In the 1960s the Communists maintained their forces in the jungles of Southern Thailand, striking across the border in minor engagements. Far to the south the integration of Sabah and Sarawak into the new Malaysia brought Indonesian aid to dissidents in Borneo.

The Chinese-indigenous population ratio of Malaysia is markedly different from that found in the rest of Southeast Asia. Instead of a small "pariah" community, the Chinese compose 3.6 million as against 4.5 million

[30] See Felix Gagliano, 1970.

[31] There are various studies of the "Emergency." One example is O'Ballance, 1966. In the "Emergency," 6,710 Communists, 1,366 Malayan police, 519 military, and 2,473 civilians were killed.

for the Malays out of the country's 10.1 million population. The Chinese themselves are cleaved by place of origin, dialect, economic class, guild, and occupation, and the Malays have their aristocracy, peasantry, and landlord class. However, as in our other cases, the two groups are divided, or perceived to be divided, along two coinciding communal and class lines. First, the two races have tended to live in separate areas. In 1957, 70 percent of the rural population of Malaya was Malay and 17 percent Chinese, whereas the urban ratio was almost the opposite. Eighty percent of urban Peninsula Malay lives in cities of 20,000 or over, none of which has a Malay majority.[32] The races are also segmented by religion, culture, history, language, and life-style.

Economically, the Chinese as a group have maintained both higher incomes and more skilled occupations. Aggregate Chinese income has been approximately two-and-a-half times that of the Malays and disparities have remained in spite of increases in Malay incomes since independence.[33] Occupationally, the Chinese have dominated mining, manufacturing, retail trades, skilled artisan trades, pig and poultry raising, and market gardening.[34] The Malays have been primarily agricultural, although government subsidy programs have been instituted to allow them to compete in commerce and transportation. In the period prior to the 1969 riots there had been high unemployment and poor economic conditions, particularly among the Malays—a factor noted as a major cause of the ensuing violence. Yet it would be a gross oversimplification to assume that all Chinese are skilled and well-to-do and all Malays poor farmers. In fact, a considerable proportion of the violence experienced in independent Malaysia involved Chinese youths from lower economic levels.

An important reason for Chinese dissatisfaction has been that their economic power has not been reflected in a commensurate political strength.

[32] Silcock and Fisk, 1963, p. 85; and Enloe, 1967, p. 38.

[33] Silcock and Fisk, 1963, pp. 2–3; on p. 5 the authors state that many Chinese "firmly believe that their wealth and Malay poverty are the natural consequences of Chinese industry, thrift and adaptability to modern ways, and of Malay indolence, thriftlessness and conservatism."

[34] See Purcell, 1957, and Enloe, 1967, pp. 45–46. Rounding Miss Enloe's figures, selected occupations in 1957 were:

Occupation	Malays	Chinese
Agriculture	573,000	101,000
Manufacturing	27,000	98,000
Commerce	32,000	127,000
Government Services	18,000	5,000
Police, Home Guard		
Prisons	44,000	5,000
Armed Forces	9,000	1,000

Table 4–1   Communal Distribution of Political Power at Various Levels in 1959 *

Communal Group	Popula- tion %	Elector- ate %	Constitu- encies %	Seats %	Cabinet appts. %
Malays	49	57	63.5	64	67
Chinese	38	36	36.5	27	25
Indians	12	7		9	8

* Source: K. J. Ratman, Communalism and the Political Process in Malaya (Kuala Lumpur: University of Malaya Press, 1965), p. 207.

Since independence the country has been governed by the Malay-dominated Alliance Party, which has granted special rights and subsidies to the Malays. They have received more secondary school and university scholarships, more subsidies for agricultural and business enterprises, the establishment of Islam as the state religion and Malay as the national language, and special voting rights. The Chinese, on their part, have felt deprived of equal political representation, a complaint borne out by the statistics in Table 4–1. Add to these figures a nine-to-one Malay majority in the police, home guard, prison personnel, and army.

The Malaysian pattern has thus been one of Chinese economic power and Malay political strength. The stereotypes of the two communities have been even more significant contributing factors. In the words of one observer of the 1969 riots:

There is a widespread perception of "relative deprivation" in each of Malaysia's major ethnic communities; amidst the Malays it is primarily economic, among the Chinese it is primarily political.[35] (emphasis in original)

It is such perceptions as these, reinforced by objective disparities, that have increased communal tensions.

The communal-class division in the United States does not necessitate elucidation here. It has been described in detail in other studies. Black Americans have complained, like their Catholic counterparts in Northern Ireland, that the majority population and its government have displayed bias in employment, education, housing, social relations, the administration of justice, and political opportunities. Like Ireland, violence has simmered for centuries, breaking out from time to time over the years. However, while the issues surrounding these conflicts have been of vital concern to both polities, casualties in recent years have been quite low.

[35] Gagliano, 1970, pp. 3–4.

To protagonists in the struggle in either Ireland or the United States, our constant references to the low level of violence must seem disconcerting. However, this chapter has analyzed violence in its worldwide context, and the number killed in each of the last three cases can be seen to be small when it is compared with perhaps a thousand times more deaths in Indonesia, China, Cambodia, Pakistan, India, Nigeria, and Colombia in the postwar years.

A question that cannot be easily answered is why these three instances have not erupted into large-scale violence. All of the elements would appear to be present—especially the reality or the perception of economic, political, and social disparity between two distinct antagonistic communal groups. Yet in each example the authorities decided to maintain order in a comparatively objective fashion; that is, they did not either turn their faces from the conflict and allow the weak to be massacred, as in Rwanda and rural Indonesia, or actively engage in the widespread killing of domestic opposition, as in all five of the high-casualty cases discussed. Part of the answer undoubtedly lies in the values, power, and political judgments of the establishment. In Northern Ireland, Malaysia, and the United States the authorities kept total deaths to less than 1,000—a comparatively good record, given the tensions present. At the same time, the populace self-regulated its actions and did not attempt to partake in the general massacre perpetrated in other parts of the world by people in similar situations. The reasons for this self-discipline can be noted only in imprecise and obscure phrases such as legitimacy, tolerance, political maturity, and self-control. Partial explanations will be investigated in the next two chapters.

That Burmans can develop and in the past have developed a comparatively high standard of social conduct is clear to anyone who has visited the remote parts of the province. It is equally clear that under modern conditions, this standard of conduct has largely disappeared. . . . The . . . reinforcements of the social interest which every society has devised . . . are . . . custom, religion, and criminal law. The Government of Burma relied almost entirely on the last named, and it is the decay of the first two that I would largely attribute the present tendencies to crime.

British Report, 1914

Basic to an understanding of the relationships of the Thai people to their king and government is an appreciation of the great respect the people accorded their official superiors.

W. Vella

LEGITIMACY AND VIOLENCE 5

The question of legitimacy is one that has plagued political theorists for centuries and this chapter certainly will not settle it. We will however try to show that low levels of violence are positively correlated with the legitimacy of institutions which support the total society. Some writers argue that the legitimacy of a regime is a sufficient condition for the minimization of violence.[1] Here it is proposed that a better correlation can be made by analyzing the combination of institutions that foster societal legitimacy rather than "regime legitimacy" alone. If respect for and loyalty to several of these fundamental social institutions are weakened, then the probability of political violence will be greatly increased.

Unfortunately, there are no extensive cross-national studies of this more complex phenomena.[2] Therefore, in this chapter we shall approach the problem by analyzing two states which scholars of Southeast Asia often have treated comparatively in the past, Burma and Thailand. This type of case study can display some of the nuances and subtleties associated with violence, and thus can illuminate factors that aggregate analysis often obscures.

These countries are roughly similar in size, climate, population, and dependence on agriculture (particularly rice); both are riverine states with histories related to major river systems; both follow Theravada Buddhism and contain small religious minorities. Furthermore, historically there have been religious, political, cultural, and military interchanges that have provided a degree of cross-fertilization. The tendency of some observers is to note these similarities, and then to explain political differences on the basis of variations both in nineteenth-century leadership and in colonial experi-

[1] See Gurr, 1970, p. 185.

[2] Gurr, 1968, pp. 1104–24, and Bwy, 1968, pp. 17–66.

ence. This chapter argues that the latter factor in particular explains the destruction of the legitimacy of traditional Burmese institutions and the resultant high level of violence, whereas the continuous independence of Thailand is in large part the reason for that country's relatively peaceful recent history.

Before commencing this analysis, it is necessary to describe the types of political violence in the two states and to assess more carefully the validity of the assertion that such conflict has been more prevalent in Burma than in Thailand. We may begin comparing Burma and Thailand according to some of the categories of violence referred to in Chapter 1.

PRIMORDIAL AND SEPARATIST VIOLENCE

Both countries have experienced primordial violence, but Burma's history has been far more difficult. In the Thai case there has been low-level violence directed against the Chinese minority and a simmering conflict in Southern Thailand involving Malay-Moslems. It was only in the 1960s that high numbers of casualties were reported in the insurgencies in North and Northeast Thailand. Both of these outbreaks were in border areas and were a mixture of ethnic, ideological, and local political issues. Religious strife has been largely absent from Thailand and only the Thai-Moslem conflict has contained important secessionist demands. In contrast, Burma has been far less homogeneous than Thailand and has suffered through half a century of religious and ethnic violence.[3] During the interwar period, Indian and Chinese minorities were targets of attacks by the local population, the bloodiest of which were primarily racially oriented but with growing nationalist overtones. The most noteworthy incidents were the anti-Indian riots of 1930, when some 100 were killed and over 1,000 injured; the anti-Chinese riots of 1931; and the extensive anti-Muslim demonstrations of 1938, when over 1,000 were killed or injured. During World War II the Christian minority was the object of persecution by Burmese Buddhists, and for more than twenty years since Burma attained independence in 1948 the country has been divided by civil war. These struggles have involved ethnic minorities including Mons, Karens, Shans, Chins, Kachins, and Arakanese. The Karen case in particular had both ethnic and religious ramifications, as every ethnic group sought greater autonomy and, in the Shan and Karen conflicts, actual separation from the Union. Total casualties from the decades of civil war are unknown but number in the thousands.

[3] For a lengthier description of the history of violence in Burma, see the chapter "Civil Strife in Burma" in Anderson, von der Mehden, and Young, 1967, pp. 98–108.

COUP AND
REVOLUTIONARY
VIOLENCE

When we compare the role of organized violence in efforts to overthrow the governments of Thailand and Burma we tread on shaky ground. There is little difficulty in dealing with certain broad aspects of the problem. Thailand has been blessed with a comparatively peaceful history as far as rural rebellion is concerned. The prewar period was almost totally devoid of major activities of this sort and the postwar era has seen extensive insurgency only since the fall of 1965. Burma's experiences have been quite different. The Saya San Rebellion against British rule in 1930–31, for which there is no counterpart in Thailand, resulted in some 3,000 casualties. We need not spend time describing the attempts by Communists, dissident military units, and ethnic groups to overthrow the Burmese government. Such attempts at organized revolutionary violence in Burma surpassed those in Thailand in numbers involved, years of conflict, and size of the geographic areas concerned.

Less clear-cut is the comparison of the experiences of the two states in efforts at political coup and assassination. The two "coups" of 1958 and 1962 instigated by the Burmese military resulted in only one death and that was not premeditated. Thailand also has experienced its share of largely bloodless attempted coups in 1932, 1938, 1944, 1947, 1948, 1950, 1952, 1957, and 1958.[4] In these cases, as in the Burmese "coups," it can be argued that the lack of violence resulted primarily from either the ability of the authorities to control the situation before violence erupted or the weakness or lack of will of the government to counter the successful conspirators. There were, however, two coup attempts in Thailand, 1949 and 1951, which resulted in comparatively large-scale violence. The February 1949 revolt in Bangkok was sharply put down and the conspirators killed. Again in 1951 an abortive coup led to more than 300 casualties. Both efforts involved aspects of interservice rivalry, which may explain the violent nature of the conflicts inasmuch as it is a factor present in other bloody coups.

In addition to coup and revolutionary violence, we should take some note of the existence of political assassination. The most prominent examples were the killing of the Burmese leader General Aung San and part of his cabinet in 1947 and the later assassination of U Tin Tut, another cabinet member. Both countries have experienced the killing of local officials and politicians. During the early years of the Communist-led insurgency in Northeast Thailand, perhaps more than 100 local leaders were killed each year.[5]

---

[4] See Wilson, 1962.

[5] Pye, 1962, notes that there were 10 to 75 noninsurgency-related political murders in Burma annually.

**ISSUE-
ORIENTED
VIOLENCE**

Compared to Thailand, Burma also has displayed more varied and serious forms of violence involving specific issues. Prior to World War II there were low-casualty strikes and student demonstrations against the colonial regime. The issues included tax policies, the alienation of land, the pace of de-colonization, and a myriad of other causes. This pattern was maintained in the postwar period when rebellions broke out over a host of specific issues, when elections normally were accompanied by local violence, and when conflict between the military and university students led to the death of a number of the latter.

Thailand also has suffered from specific issue-oriented political violence. Experiencing less foreign land expropriation, uninvolved in nationalist emotions against colonialism, and less concerned with tax issues, there were fewer issues to motivate political violence, but anomic disturbances with political overtones could be found throughout the kingdom. The specific issues related to such circumstances as local official corruption, illegal opium, spirits or timber cutting, and elections. On balance it appears that this type of political violence has been more prevalent in Burma.

Any meaningful comparison of violence in the two countries must set the phenomena of political violence against the backdrop of crime differentials. Colonial Burma was described as having the highest crime rate in the British Empire. Theft was three-and-a-half times that of India and in 1940 the per capita murder rate was more than five times greater than the Indian average.[6] By the year before the war the rate had climbed even higher. In comparison, Thailand's crime statistics showed far fewer reported crimes.

It is particularly difficult to judge the political relevance of crime during periods of fast modernization, growing nationalism, and inadequate police observation. In Burma the relation of dacoity (banditry) to anti-foreign nationalism led a noted historian on Burma to remark that, "Criminal elements were thus able to circulate in good patriotic company."[7] There is no question that violent crime increased at the same time as did political

---

[6] Christian, 1945, p. 159. It should be noted that many of the Indians brought into Burma in the nineteenth century were from the "criminal class" and that in 1875–77 the Indian jail population was four-and-a-half times that of the Burmese Buddhists. This ratio soon changed to a majority of Burmese. See also Furnivall, 1948.

[7] Cady, 1958, p. 275. It was also the view of a conservative interwar commission appointed to study problems of stability in the province. See the excellent OSS study, *The Problem of Law and Order in Burma Under British Administration*, 1944, p. 66. This is the best study of violence in prewar Burma. It should also be noted that nationalist organizations had the most strength in Tharawaddy and Prome, noted for high crime.

agitation. Certain types of violence associated with rural protests against land taxes, the alienation of land, unpopular police practices, and nationalism were encouraged by some nationalist political leaders.

In sum then, there is little doubt that society-initiated violence has been a more frequent occurrence in Burma. The obvious question that now arises is why? Two major concepts have been presented over the years to explain Burmese violence in general. These are the breakdown of authority under the impact of British colonialism and arguments based more upon deep-seated behavioral traits of the Burmese.[8] The importance of the first factor cannot be overemphasized; it is crucial to any understanding of Burmese violence. Four aspects of the breakdown of authority in Burma, largely lacking in Thailand, should be noted.

---

1. AUTHORITY OF THE STATE AND COLONIAL SYSTEM

The imposition of the British colonial system on Burma and its destruction of traditional authority patterns brought laws, administration, and policies which lacked familiarity and legitimacy. The Burma which initially confronted the British was not a collapsing empire such as the colonial intruders found in China and the East Indies. Although weakened by monarchical mistakes and corrupt in its administration, an aggressive Burma had sacked the Thai capital of Ayudthya in 1767 and the first Anglo-Burmese War was in large part due to Burmese designs on Manipur, Assam, Chahar, and other parts of eastern India.[9] Thus, the humiliating defeats of the nation during the nineteenth century must have been traumatic in their implications. There is no question that there were Burmese still living in the 1920s and 1930s who personally remembered the old monarchical authority system and romanticized its loss. Furthermore, various politicians did not allow the people to forget the legitimate role of the former government in contrast to the colonial regime.[10]

The colonial experience resulted in a breakdown of state authority and legitimacy on several administrative levels. At the top, the Burmese initially were not given major positions of authority in the national administration when the old court and monarchy were eliminated.[11] Leadership

---

[8] See Furnivall, 1948, and Pye, 1962.

[9] For a Burmese view of this period and the British occupation, see Maung Htin Aung, 1967 and 1965. For a European view see Cady, 1958. For an excellent Thai comparison of Burma and Thailand, see Sirisumpundh, 1962.

[10] See, for example, the Burma Round Table Conference, 1932. A number of politicians at these meetings discussed the loss of power and status under the British occupation.

[11] See Donnison, 1970, pp. 67–92.

was foreign in personnel, lacked traditional legitimacy, and remained largely Christian in a society that came to romanticize the religious aspects of the old kingdom. Furthermore, the colonial administrator often displayed his conviction of the racial superiority of the British and did not make sufficient efforts to ascertain Burmese needs. Thus even while local youths attacked colonial education as irrelevant to traditional national life, they saw the necessity of obtaining a foreign education in order to advance in the new society. These Burmese entrants into the colonial bureaucracy often mimicked the British, further alienating the masses.

Thailand, in contrast was ruled by a succession of able kings who provided traditional religious and political continuity and loyalty.[12] Thai rulers were aware of the inroads of colonialism in Burma and China, so that Westernization took place under the supervision of the monarchy. Although the regime was cautious about permitting change, reforms were promulgated at all levels. Initially the bureaucracy remained largely semi-hereditary and indigenously educated. Where change in Burma was carried out by Western colonial bureaucrats, in Thailand it was limited by an insufficient number of educated leaders; even foreign advisors were carefully supervised. Thus, an attack on the state in Thailand could be construed as a combined act of treason, lèse majesté, and sacrilege, whereas to the Burmese it could be termed an act of patriotism and a defense of Buddhism.

Even more importantly, the British colonial administration destroyed the traditional village and legal systems and substituted patterns lacking both legitimacy and familiarity in the eyes of the villager. Varied British commentators had noted earlier that the village in monarchical Burma had provided stability to the system. Local headmen had been men of status who enjoyed considerable authority. Under the colonial administration headmen were appointed by British deputy commissioners and were responsible to them. This tie with the foreigner made it difficult for the headmen to maintain their social leadership. By making the new headman a combined tax collector, policeman, and petty magistrate, the colonial power put a man in the village who was outwardly supported by the foreign authority of the colonial administration but who lacked legitimacy in the mind of the villager. Law became unfamiliar and litigation expanded as lawyers took advantage of the situation. The result was local administration that became incapable of handling the fast-changing pattern of Burmese rural life as the money economy and nationalism intruded into the countryside.

Again, Thailand was markedly different from Burma at the local and provincial levels. Although major administrative changes were made under the leadership of King Chulalongkorn and Prince Damrong, they were

---

[12] See Vella, 1955, and Rabibhadana, 1969.

formulated within the Thai context, by Thai officials, and with royal legitimacy.[13] Secondly, these changes developed comparatively slowly and the village retained considerable local authority to choose its leaders, always with at least veto power in the hands of the district officer. Village government therefore remained familiar and indigenous.

2. AUTHORITY OF THE RELIGIOUS HIERARCHY

The king and *sangha* (Buddhist monkhood) were both important integrating forces in precolonial Burma that the British administration consciously and unconsciously damaged through its policies.[14] This deterioration was experienced in a variety of ways.

First, the manner in which Burma was occupied by the colonial power —that is, through three territorial stages of conquest—led to the disintegration of central hierarchical control. As the British occupation moved north, the *sangha* no longer came under the de facto authority of the faction-ridden hierarchy in areas lost to the monarchy. Secondly, when the colonial administration put the *sangha* under secular law and discipline in the latter part of the nineteenth century, central ecclesiastical disciplinary power was all but eliminated. Finally, the colonial environment demanded Western education in English rather than training in traditional subjects and Pali as provided in the monastery schools. This led to an increased call for missionary-taught education and a drastic diminution of monastery school enrollments.[15]

The aforementioned factors produced two results that were deleterious to public order. First, it weakened one more traditional bulwark of authority providing legitimacy to the system and sanctioning the rules by which men lived. Secondly, it weakened disciplinary power over the *sangha* at a time when many of its members were becoming politicized by the perceived threat to Buddhist institutions and culture posed by the British administration. An appreciable number of monks became political activists undeterred by religious prohibitions against secular involvement; they functioned as leaders and participants in both prewar and postwar violent political demonstrations.

Again, the comparison with Thailand is striking. In Thailand the Buddhist hierarchy remained intact, with the king closely associated in the popular mind with religious authority. In the absence of perceived major perils to Buddhist institutions and culture, symbolized by the Christian

[13] Steinberg, et al., 1971, pp. 113ff.

[14] See von der Mehden, 1963.

[15] See von der Mehden, forthcoming.

colonial government in Burma, the *sangha* remained apolitical. This provided the government with legitimacy and deprived opponents of both a volatile issue and ready-made local leadership. Even today the Communists find it difficult to attack the ideological trinity of Buddhism, King, and Country.

---

3. POPULATION DISPLACEMENT AND LAND ALIENATION

The opening of the Suez Canal and the consolidation of European power in Asia acted as twin catalysts bringing a rapid expansion of commercial agriculture to Southeast Asia. In both Burma and Thailand new lands were opened, rice production expanded, and the money economy penetrated more deeply into the rural areas. The impact of these developments was more rapid and the results more traumatic in Burma, however. The British opened the Burmese economy to a freewheeling laissez-faire system and the colony's agricultural production and exports jumped as vast tracts of Lower Burma were cleared for rice. Acreage under rice in these frontier lands of Lower Burma expanded from 1 million in 1855 after the second Anglo-Burmese War to 2 million in 1873 and thereafter by an average of approximately 1 million every seven years until the depression.[16] The Burmese, however, did not perceive this development as profiting the indigenous population. The new commercial farmers, complaining of high taxes, the alienation of land, usury, and crime, were quick to lay the blame on foreigners, particularly the Indian moneylenders and British colonial government.

The Burmese tillers were largely unused to modern commercial agriculture and soon fell prey to Indian moneylenders and rentiers who often charged usurious rates and high rents. When the Indians foreclosed on Burmese unable to pay loans or taxes, land alienation increased to major proportions. By 1928, 42 percent of the agricultural land of Lower Burma was held by tenants, a figure that rose to 58 percent in 1935 under the impact of the depression.[17] Along with this alienation of land to foreign absentee landlords went seasonal unemployment, rack-renting, and strong

---

[16] Steinberg et al., 1971, p. 223. Figures of acreage under rice in Lower Burma show the following:

1830	66,000
1860	1,333,000
1890	4,398,000
1900	6,578,000
1910	7,808,000
1920	8,588,000
1930	9,111,000

[17] See Burmese government, 1949.

anti-Indian and anti-foreign sentiment. The colonization of Lower Burma thus brought with it the formation of new villages, lacking roots, based upon a money economy and under pressure from the colonial administrator and Indian moneylenders. These villages appear to have been particularly prone to growing rates of crime and politically related rural disturbances. It is interesting to note that in Upper Burma and the Shan states, where land alienation did not proceed as rapidly and where authority was less disrupted, political violence and crime were less prevalent.

Comparing Thai agricultural development to Burmese, we may note that the Thai rice industry maintained a steady growth to World War II. Expansion of new rice lands was slower, increasing from 5.8 million rai in 1850 to 9.1 million in 1905/6, to 20.1 million in 1930, a less than threefold increase as against a ninefold multiplication in Burma during the same period.[18] This more cautious development in part resulted from financial strictures on the fast development of irrigation and drainage and the smaller input of outside capital. In fact, in sharp contrast with the Burmese experience, the expansion of Thai commercial agriculture was largely in the hands of the indigenous rural population and Chinese credit was on the whole less important than Thai. Thus when the depression hit there was no serious passage of land to aliens and the ratio of tenants to landowners was lower than in Burma.[19]

Although certainly Burma displayed a greater frequency of violence than did Thailand in the prewar period, there were several aspects of the Japanese occupation of Burma which aided the proliferation of political conflicts in the postwar years. First, the central government in Burma authority lost its monopoly of arms, thus allowing dissident groups to compete more equally in terms of armed violence. The training and arming of the Burmese nationalist forces by the Japanese and similar efforts by the allies among the hill tribes enabled such disparate groups as the military dissidents, ethnic rebels, Communists, and assassins of Aung San to assault the governmental structure in both rural and urban areas more effectively.

Secondly, the years of guerrilla and more traditional warfare, which started in 1941 and which still continue in a sporadic fashion, provided several generations of young men with little experience outside an environment of violence. The Japanese period alone left its residue of dissident,

---

[18] Ingram, 1955, pp. 43–44.

[19] Zimmerman, 1931, p. 18. This is a good analysis of Thai agriculture at the time of the depression.

armed, politicized, and partially trained youth who later joined a variety of rebellions.

Thirdly, the occupation by the Japanese brought into question the legitimacy of three other groups who had lent strength, albeit sporadically, to the political order of prewar Burma. The British administration, lost "face" in the eyes of the populace because of its inability to defend the colony. Thus their defeat made difficult if not impossible the reimposition of British rule in Burma. Furthermore, the flight of senior Burmese civil servants to India ahead of the advancing Japanese undermined confidence in their effectiveness and loyalty. Finally, the character of wartime rule by the older politicians who cooperated with the Japanese was such as to make a whole generation of political leaders at least suspect. Thus the wartime leader, Dr. Ba Maw, and his followers were accused by younger nationalists of autocratic and ostentatious rule. As a result, the imposition of Japanese authority weakened the legitimacy of other foundationstones of societal legitimacy while making it easier for dissidents to develop armed opposition.

On these points the experiences of Thailand were significantly at variance with those of Burma. Thailand was not officially occupied and controls were disguised as "mutual cooperation in all fields whether it be military, economic, or cultural." [20] The kingdom maintained intact its monarchical, administrative, and military structures (although the young King Ananda remained in Switzerland during the war). Basically, there was little Japanese control below the top and the administration in Bangkok remained in authority in the rural areas to the extent it previously had, with relatively few unimportant exceptions. The Thai military had strong traditional roots and the war did not engender any significant radicalization or further politicization of the ranks. The anti-Japanese Free Thai Movement did not engage in large-scale arming or training of dissidents, and many of its leaders later took important places in the government. In other words, Thailand was the least influenced by the war of all the Southeast Asian states and had the easiest transition to peacetime rule and economic recovery.

SUMMARY

If we briefly analyze the results of the relative loss of legitimacy and authority in Burma, it is possible to isolate four primary factors which abetted political violence. First, authority in colonial Burma was neither familiar nor acceptable to most politicized Burmese, and thus did not contain within it recognized sanctions to the extent

[20] United States, Office of Strategic Services, 1944, Japanese Domination of Thailand, p. 5.

that it did in the more traditionally based Thai Kingdom. Particularly in the period immediately after the final occupation of the Burmese Kingdom and the growth of modern nationalism, nationalistic and religious brands of political violence against the colonial government received support from important elements of Burmese society. Secondly, religious authority was weakened by colonial rule and modernization leading to the dual losses of *sangha* discipline and the spiritual foundation to the new polity. Thirdly, economic change and dislocation developed more rapidly in Burma and the gains of modernization appeared to go into alien hands. Finally, with the Japanese occupation and the instability of postwar Burma, the government was physically incapable of containing those who chose to employ armed force. Meanwhile, the Thai system was maintained with only incremental changes resulting in the retention of order and a virtual monopoly of force in the hands of the Thai leadership. Thus when violence did assert itself within Thailand it was normally a result of conflicts within the leadership rather than a result of social tensions.

Our examination in this chapter of some of the factors which have led to more frequent political violence in Burma almost forces us to conclude that Thailand can look forward to increased conflict in the future. Some contemporary Thai similarities to former Burmese experiences include:

1. In Northeast Thailand the present insurgency has been at least partially successful in undermining the legitimacy of government through the assassination of its personnel, defiance of its laws, and attacks on traditional institutions.

2. Modernization and urbanization of the society is seriously threatening traditional authority structures such as the family and the Buddhist hierarchy.

3. Foreign support of the present Thai government allows opponents to accuse it of being an agent of imperialism and an enemy of Thai nationalism.

4. Training and arms provided to the insurgents from the outside have broken the Thai government's practical monopoly in modern means of violence.

. . . want is the enemy of peace and hopelessness—the mother of violence. . . . The wealthy nations cannot survive as islands of abundance in a world of hunger, sickness, and despair.

Lyndon B. Johnson, 1967

SOCIAL AND ECONOMIC CONDITIONS AND POLITICAL VIOLENCE

6

With Kim Q. Hill

INTRODUCTION: DATA AND METHODOLOGY

Through the postwar years an underlying principle of American foreign aid and part of our "conventional wisdom" regarding poverty and violence has been the belief that there is a direct relationship between low economic and social levels on the one hand and violence on the other. All sorts of people —including U.S. Congressmen—believe that violence and Communism feed upon people who are poor, underfed, and undereducated, and that it is only necessary to raise those standards in order to achieve peace and democracy. From this central thought a number of more sophisticated arguments have been suggested: increased development results in greater support to the indigenous government, thus producing a more stable system; development brings larger sections of the population into the money economy, thus giving them a greater stake in the system and making them less vulnerable to those preaching violence; sustained economic growth will increase the viability of political and social institutions, thus creating the bases for stable democratic governments or at least establishing institutions more capable of meeting the grievances of disadvantaged power groups. These hypotheses all add up to what Princeton Lyman disparagingly calls the "candy bar theory" that political loyalty can be achieved by appropriate gifts.

Recently, a number of critics have begun severely questioning these economic determinist arguments. For example, the prestigious Pearson Commission on International Development stated: "Development is not a guarantee of political stability or an antidote to violence. Change is, itself, intrinsically disruptive." [1] Yet even while we are beginning to recognize the

[1] Department of State, 1966, pp. 874–81.

complexities of violence and to be more cautious in applying outmoded theories of economic determinism to the developing world, the old arguments have crept into apologias for programs formulated in the United States to meet domestic violence. Former Attorney-General Ramsey Clark reflected this attitude in his book *Crime in America:*

> *Most crime in America is born in environments saturated in poverty and its consequences: illness, ugly surroundings, hopelessness. . . .*
>   *The solutions for our slums, for racism and crime itself in mass society, are primarily economic. . . . If we are to control crime, we must undertake a massive effort to rebuild our cities and ourselves, to improve the human condition, to educate, employ, house and make healthy.*[2]

While we do not deny that a relationship exists between economic and social deprivation and political violence, we seek in this chapter to delineate the character of the relationships cross-nationally using available aggregate data. In this way we may have a test of Robert McNamara's assertion that "there is a direct and constant relationship between the incidence of violence and the economic status and social position of the countries afflicted."[3]

For the purpose of this analysis we chose from each geocultural region of the world the four most and least violent nations, thus making possible comparisons between relatively violent and quiescent nations, both on a regional and a worldwide basis. Because domestic violence has a number of dimensions, it is probably not possible to devise a single country-rating scheme that would account for all instances. However, an effort was made to single out those countries with the highest and lowest incidence of domestic violence in terms of events and casualties between 1950 and 1965 (1960–69 for Sub-Saharan Africa).[4]

[2] Clark, 1970, pp. 57 and 67.

[3] McNamara, 1966, pp. 874–81.

[4] The violence data used in this study were the Feierabends' "Cross-National Data Bank of Political Instability Events" for 1948–1965 (from the Interuniversity Consortium for Political Research); a scaling method utilized by Betty Nesvold and the Feierabends was deemed suitable. The technique was twofold. First, *violent* events from the Feierabend data set were cast into a four-point Guttman-like scale of the intensity of violence (based on the occurrence of particular types of violence events). Second, individual nations were given a scale score for each analysis year based upon the type and number of violent events reported therein. The scale scores were then accumulated for each state over the entire analysis period (1950–1965 for the original Feierabend nations and 1960–1969 for the Sub-Saharan African nations added for this study). Because the Feierabend data do not include Sub-Saharan African nations, event data for these nations were collected according to the Feierabend criteria and sources, and then each of these nations were similarly scored. The nations chosen for

The nations thus chosen for the analysis were:

	Europe	Asia	Latin Amer.	N. Africa	Sub-Saharan Africa
Low Vio- lence	Denmark Finland Netherlands New Zealand	Cambodia Japan Malaya China (T)	Costa Rica El Salvador Uruguay Ecuador	Afghanistan Saudi Arabia Israel Libya	Mali Somali Upper Volta Zambia
High Vio- lence	France Portugal Spain USSR	India Indonesia S. Korea S. Vietnam	Argentina Bolivia Cuba Venezuela	Iran Iraq Sudan Syria	Cameroon Congo (K) Ghana Nigeria

It should be noted that this data showed "advanced" nations in both the highest and lowest levels of the violence ratings, although as a group the European states ranked the lowest of any of the regions surveyed in violent events.

A number of very serious caveats must be emphasized when considering these data. Before we proceed with our analysis, we should alert the reader to some defects or possibly misleading aspects of the technique we are using here. For example, nations with a few high-intensity violent events will be placed lower than nations with a large number of low-level experiences. Thus, Rwanda is not listed as a high-violence case in spite of more deaths than Cameroon, where there were a large number of executions but considerably fewer deaths and far less destruction. In Europe, Hungary ranks far below the high-violence states in the list, although the 1956 revolt was probably the bloodiest event in postwar Europe.

Furthermore, because of the ever-present problem of poor reporting, some states are not ranked as they might have been if more data had been available. Thus, the data base used here does not place Colombia among the four highest-violence Latin American cases, although some experts report that approximately 200,000 were killed over several years in inter-party conflict; similarly, Burma would have ranked far higher if consideration had been given to other data on the generation-long civil war which

the original scaling were generally those in the Feierabend set (excluding Iceland because of its small population and South Africa because of a suspiciously high score resulting from a very high incidence of reported events of low violence levels) plus Sub-Saharan nations with a population of two million or more by 1968 and independence no later than 1965.

has racked that country since 1947. On the other hand, violence in Western states, where there are better communications and a more interested reading public, appears more regularly in the files used in this technique.

A third problem arises because this listing does not take into account events transpiring before 1948 and after 1965, except in the Sub-Saharan African case which cover the years 1960 to 1969. It thus may appear strange that Cambodia is included as a low-violence case and that Pakistan is not included in the high-violence list. However, the necessity of maintaining consistency and the absence of reliable data for current activities were controlling factors in our choice of chronological limits.

Finally, there were cases where, in the judgment of the authors, the event data could not be employed because it contradicted our own evaluation of the level of violence in the particular state. Thus Rwanda scored lowest of all the African states in spite of 10,000 to 14,000 killed in massacres in the early 1960s, South Africa scored highest of all states due primarily to insignificant incidents, and Communist China ranked the fourth lowest of all Asian nations in spite of the political trials of 1950–52, the Tibetan civil war, and the admitted killing of political agents of the government of Taiwan (which is a domestic issue by the standards of the Chinese Communists). In sum, while we are generally satisfied that the listing includes cases from the highest- and lowest-violence states in each region, we recognize that strong arguments can be made for considering other countries and do not regard the data as sufficiently reliable for allowing us to rank states within the categories established.

After tabulating the data to generate the list of states given above, these states were then correlated with twelve economic and social variables in order to establish whether there exists a significant relationship between violence and economic-social levels.[5] These were:

I. ECONOMIC DEVELOPMENT

A. Electricity Production (MW) per Capita, 1955 & 1965

B. National Income per Capita, 1955 & 1965

C. Total Government Expenditure per Capita, 1955 & 1965

D. Agricultural Population (Percent of Work Force), 1965

[5] The bulk of the socioeconomic data used in this study was provided by George Antunes from material collected from his dissertation. See Antunes, 1971. In cases where data were outdated or missing, reference was made to more current United Nations publications or the original sources themselves to update data and fill in the gaps.

II. COMMUNICATIONS AND EDUCATION

    A. Telephones per Thousand Population, 1955 & 1965

    B. Radios per Thousand Population, 1955 & 1965

    C. Newspaper Circulation per Thousand Population, 1955 & 1965

    D. Illiteracy Rate (percent), 1965

III. SOCIETAL AND POLITICAL

    A. Ethno-Linguistic Fractionalization

    B. Separatist Potential

    C. Armed Forces as Percent of Population, 1965

    D. Security Forces per Ten Thousand Population, 1965

All of the caveats presented in Chapter 1 on the use of violence data need to be underlined when considering economic and social data, particularly when dealing with developing nations. However, every effort was made to insure the accuracy of the statistics upon which the tables used in this chapter were based. Although the authors are not totally satisfied with all the data presented, they believe that the data provide the basis for some tentative conclusions.

ECONOMIC DEVELOPMENT DATA

Levels of political violence were significant correlated with economic statistics only in Europe; in Asia there was a specific correlation between violence and the agricultural indices among our economic variables. In the European cases low violence tended to coincide with higher per capita electricity production, national income, and government expenditures. However, this pattern tended to become less apparent over time, so that France and the USSR—high-violence states—were also on the higher end of the economic scale. In the Asian statistics a higher percentage of agricultural workers tended to be correlated with high-violence countries. For the rest of the regions analyzed, no significant relationships were brought out by the data. Thus for the countries of the survey as a whole (with the possible exception of European countries) it cannot be argued that evidence supports McNamara's conclusion regarding the coincidence of violence and economic status within geographic areas.

Table 6–1   1955 Electricity Production (MW) per Capita

	0–0.5 MW	0.5–1.0	1.0–2.0	2.0–
Low		Denmark	Finland Netherlands	New Zealand
High	Portugal Spain	USSR	France	
Low	Cambodia China (T) Malaya	Japan		
High	India Indonesia South Korea Vietnam			
Low	Costa Rica Ecuador El Salvador Uruguay			
High	Argentina Bolivia Cuba			
Low	Afghanistan Libya	Israel		
High	Iran Iraq Sudan Syria			
Low	Somali			
High	Cameroon Congo (K)			

Table 6–2 1965 Electricity Production (MW) per Capita

	0–0.5 MW	0.5–1.0	1.0–2.0	2.0–
Low			Denmark	Finland Netherlands New Zealand
High		Portugal Spain		France USSR
Low	Cambodia Malaya	China (T)	Japan	
High	India Indonesia South Korea Vietnam			
Low	Costa Rica Ecuador El Salvador	Uruguay		
High	Bolivia Cuba	Argentina Venezuela		
Low	Afghanistan Libya Saudi Arabia		Israel	
High	Iran Iraq Sudan Syria			
Low	Somali			
High	Cameroon Congo (K)			

Table 6–3   1955 National Income per Capita

	$0–100	101–500	501–1,000	1,001–
Low			Denmark Finland Netherlands	New Zealand
High		Spain Portugal USSR	France	
Low	Cambodia	China (T) Japan Malaya		
High	India South Korea	Indonesia South Vietnam		
Low		Costa Rica Ecuador El Salvador Uruguay		
High		Argentina Cuba Bolivia	Venezuela	
Low	Afghanistan Libya	Saudi Arabia	Israel	
High	Sudan	Iran Iraq Syria		
Low	Mali Somali Upper Volta	Zambia } all estimates		
High	Congo (K) Nigeria Cameroon	Ghana		

Table 6–4 1965 National Income per Capita

	$0–100	101–500	501–1,000	1,001–
Low				Denmark Finland Netherlands New Zealand
High		Portugal Spain	USSR	France
Low		Cambodia China (T) Malaya	Japan	
High	India South Korea	Vietnam	Indonesia	
Low	Costa Rica El Salvador	Ecuador	Uruguay (Gross Domestic Product)	
High		Bolivia (Gross Domestic Product)	Argentina Cuba Venezuela	
Low	Afghanistan	Saudi Arabia	Libya	Israel
High	Sudan	Iran Iraq Syria		
Low	Mali Somali Upper Volta	Zambia		
High	Congo (K) Nigeria	Cameroon Ghana		

Table 6–5 1955 Total Government Expenditure per Capita

	$0–50	51–150	151–300	301–
Low			Denmark Finland Netherlands New Zealand	
High	Portugal Spain		France	USSR
Low	Cambodia China (T) Japan Malaya			
High	India Indonesia South Korea Vietnam			
Low	Ecuador El Salvador	Costa Rica	Uruguay	
High	Argentina Bolivia	Cuba	Venezuela	
Low	Afghanistan Libya	Israel Saudi Arabia		
High	Iran Iraq Sudan Syria			
Low	Upper Volta Mali Somali Zambia			
High	Congo (K) Ghana Cameroon			

Table 6–6   1965 Total Government Expenditure per Capita

	$0–50	51–150	151–300	301–
Low				Denmark Finland Netherlands New Zealand
High		Portugal Spain		France USSR
Low	Cambodia China (T)	Japan Malaya		
High	India Indonesia South Korea	Vietnam		
Low	Ecuador El Salvador	Costa Rica		Uruguay
High	Bolivia	Argentina Cuba	Venezuela	
Low	Afghanistan	Saudi Arabia	Libya	Israel
High	Sudan Syria	Iran Iraq		
Low	Mali Somali Upper Volta	Zambia		
High	Cameroon Congo Nigeria	Ghana		

Table 6–7   1965 Agricultural Population (Percentage of Work Force)

	0–25%	26–50	51–75	76–
Low	Denmark Netherlands New Zealand	Finland		
High	France	Portugal USSR Spain		
Low	Japan	Malaya	China (T)	Cambodia
High			South Korea India Indonesia South Vietnam	
Low	Uruguay	Costa Rica	Ecuador El Salvador	
High	Argentina	Cuba Venezuela	Bolivia	
Low	Israel	Libya	Saudi Arabia	Afghanistan
High		Iraq	Iron Syria	Sudan
Low				Mali Somali Upper Volta Zambia
High			Ghana	Congo (K) Cameroon Nigeria

COMMUNICATIONS AND EDUCATION

We were also interested in discovering whether communications and education were significantly correlated with political violence. It can be argued that better education and the existence of greater means of communicating ideas and information should lead to greater systemic stability and lower levels of political violence. Our material does not bear out this proposition.

Three types of communications were considered—telephones, radios, and newspapers. (See Tables 6-8—6-14.) In each case we analyzed per capita possession or circulation in relation to categories of political violence. Although there were slight variations and minor relationships, particularly in Europe, overall there was little correlation between communications and the presence of violence.

Our education information also offered no support for the view that education is positively correlated with lower levels of violence. Illiteracy showed little or no regional correlation with categories of violence, with only two states—Portugal and Israel—showing any significant divergence from the norm.

SOCIETAL AND POLITICAL DATA

This section considers two politico-social elements: social divergence of groups within a state and the presence of organized security. Although these data do not relate directly to economic and social standards, it is worthy of note because of the significance of the data and the relation to what was discussed in the chapter on communal-class conflict. The data showed that there was some significant relationship between levels of political violence and the degree to which a society was ethnically and linguistically homogeneous. However, an even stronger relationship was found when we correlated violence with the percentage of regional or ethnic groups dissatisfied with the government. Postwar political conflict has certainly been based in many cases on communal and separatist issues. The case method seems to raise some interesting questions as to why so many countries with high separatist aspirations have not displayed high levels of violence.

It also can be asked whether greater government force exists as either a cause or result of levels of violence. Tables 6-15 and 6-16 deal with this matter and show considerable mixture, but no significant correlations.

In sum, with the exception of separatist potential and ethnic-linguistic divisions, no significant correlations appeared between levels of violence on the one hand and economic development, communications, education, and societal and political data on the other in all but one of the regions analyzed.

Table 6-8   1955 Telephones per Thousand Population

	0–50	51–100	101–200	201–
Low			Finland Netherlands	Denmark New Zealand
High	Portugal Spain USSR	France		
Low	Cambodia China (T) Japan Malaya			
High	India Indonesia South Korea Vietnam			
Low	Costa Rica Ecuador El Salvador Uruguay			
High	Bolivia Cuba Venezuela	Argentina		
Low	Afghanistan Libya Israel Saudi Arabia			
High	Iran Iraq Syria Sudan			
Low	Mali Somali Upper Volta Zambia			
High	Cameroon Congo (K) Ghana Nigeria			

Table 6–9 1965 Telephones per Thousand Population

	0–50	51–100	101–200	201–
Low			Finland	Denmark Netherlands New Zealand
High	USSR	Portugal Spain	France	
Low	Cambodia China (T) Malaya		Japan	
High	India Indonesia South Korea Vietnam			
Low	Costa Rica Ecuador El Salvador	Uruguay		
High	Bolivia Cuba Venezuela	Argentina		
Low	Afghanistan Libya Saudi Arabia		Israel	
High	Iran Iraq Sudan Syria			
Low	Mali Somali	Upper Volta Zambia		
High	Cameroon Congo (K) Nigeria	Ghana		

Table 6–10   1955 Radios per Thousand Population

	0–50	51–100	101–200	201–
Low				Denmark Finland Netherlands New Zealand
High		Portugal Spain	USSR	France
Low	Cambodia China Malaya		Japan	
High	India Indonesia South Korea Vietnam			
Low	Ecuador El Salvador	Costa Rica	Uruguay	
High		Bolivia	Argentina Cuba Venezuela	
Low	Afghanistan Libya Saudi Arabia		Israel	
High	Iran Iraq Syria Sudan			
Low	Mali Somali Upper Volta Zambia			
High	Cameroon Ghana Nigeria Congo (K)			

Table 6–11 1965 Radios per Thousand Population

	0–50	51–100	101–200	201–
Low				Denmark Finland Netherlands New Zealand
High			Portugal Spain	France USSR
Low	Malaya Cambodia	China (T)		Japan
High	India Indonesia Vietnam	South Korea		
Low	Ecuador	Costa Rica El Salvador		Uruguay
High			Bolivia Cuba Venezuela	Argentina
Low	Afghanistan Libya Saudi Arabia			Israel
High	Sudan	Iran		Syria Iraq
Low	Mali Somali Upper Volta Zambia			
High	Cameroon Nigeria Congo (K)	Ghana		

Table 6–12   1955 Newspaper Circulation per 1,000 Population

	0–50 copies	51–100	101–200	201–
Low				Denmark Finland Netherlands New Zealand
High		Portugal Spain		France USSR
Low	Cambodia China Malaya			Japan
High	India Indonesia Vietnam	South Korea		
Low	Ecuador El Salvador	Costa Rica	Uruguay	
High	Bolivia		Argentina Cuba Venezuela	
Low	Afghanistan Libya Saudi Arabia			Israel
High	Iran Iraq Syria Sudan			
Low	Mali Somali Upper Volta Zambia			
High	Cameroon Congo (K) Ghana Nigeria			

Table 6–13   1965 Newspaper Circulation per 1,000 Population

	0–50 copies	51–100	101–200	201–
Low				Denmark Finland Netherlands New Zealand
High		Portugal	Spain	France USSR
Low	Cambodia	China (T) Malaya		Japan
High	India Indonesia Vietnam	South Korea		
Low	Ecuador El Salvador	Costa Rica		Uruguay
High	Bolivia	Cuba Venezuela	Argentina	
Low	Afghanistan Libya Saudi Arabia		Israel	
High	Iran Iraq Sudan Syria			
Low	Mali Somali Upper Volta Zambia			
High	Cameroon Congo (K) Ghana Nigeria			

Table 6–14   1965 Illiteracy Rate (Percent)

	0–5%	6–15	16–50	51–100
Low	Denmark Finland Netherlands New Zealand			
High	France USSR	Spain	Portugal	
Low	Japan		China (T)	Cambodia Malaya
High			South Korea	India Indonesia Vietnam
Low		Uruguay	Costa Rica Ecuador	El Salvador
High	Cuba	Argentina	Venezuela	Bolivia
Low		Israel		Afghanistan Libya Saudi Arabia
High				Syria Iran Iraq Sudan
Low				Zambia Mali Somali Upper Volta
High				Cameroon Congo (K) Ghana Nigeria

Table 6–15 Ethno-Linguistic Fractionalization, 1965 *

	0–25%		26–50%		51–75%		76–100%	
Low	Costa Rica	(07)	Cambodia	(30)	Afghanistan	(66)		
	Denmark	(05)	China (T)	(35)	Ecuador	(53)		
	El Salvador	(17)	New Zealand	(37)	Malaya	(72)		
	Finland	(16)						
	Israel	(20)						
	Japan	(02)						
	Libya	(23)						
	Netherlands	(10)						
	Saudi Arabia	(06)						
	Uruguay	(20)						
High	Cuba	(04)	Argentina	(30)	Bolivia	(68)	India	(89)
	Portugal	(01)	France	(26)	Sudan	(74)	Indonesia	(76)
	South Korea	(00)	Iraq	(36)	USSR	(67)	Iran	(76)
	Syria	(22)	Spain	(44)				
	Venezuela	(11)						

* Same for all years.

Table 6–16 Separatist Potential *

	0–10%		11–20%		21–40%		41–50%	
Low	Cambodia	(5)					Afghanistan	(50)
	China (T)	(0)						
	Costa Rica	(0)						
	Denmark	(0)						
	Ecuador	(0)						
	El Salvador	(0)						
	Finland	(0)						
	Israel	(0)						
	Japan	(0)						
	Libya	(0)						
	Malaya	(0)						
	Netherlands	(0)						
	New Zealand	(0)						
	Saudi Arabia	(0)						
	South Korea	(0)						
	Uruguay	(0)						
High	Argentina	(0)	Iraq	(20)	Indonesia	(35)	India	(45)
	Bolivia	(0)	Spain	(15)	Iran	(25)	USSR	(45)
	Cuba	(0)			Sudan	(30)		
	France	(0)						
	Portugal	(0)						
	Syria	(10)						
	Venezuela	(0)						

* Same for all years.

Table 6–17   1965 Armed Forces as a Percentage of Population

	0–5	6–10	11–25	25–
Low		Finland New Zealand	Denmark Netherlands	
High		Spain	France Portugal USSR	
Low	Cambodia Japan	Malaya		China (T)
High	India Indonesia		Vietnam South Korea	
Low	Costa Rica El Salvador Uruguay	Ecuador		
High	Argentina Bolivia Venezuela	Cuba		
Low	Saudi Arabia	Afghanistan Libya		Israel
High	Sudan	Iran Iraq Syria		
Low	Mali Somali Upper Volta Zambia			
High	Cameroon Congo (K) Ghana Nigeria			

Table 6–18 1965 Security Forces per 10,000 Adult Population

	0–10	11–25	25–45	45–
Low	Finland	Denmark New Zealand	Netherlands	
High		Portugal	Spain USSR	France
Low	Cambodia	Japan	China (T)	Malaya
High		India Indonesia South Korea Vietnam		
Low	Ecuador El Salvador Uruguay	Costa Rica		
High	Argentina Bolivia Cuba Venezuela			
Low	Libya Saudi Arabia	Afghanistan	Israel	
High		Iran Sudan Syria		Iraq
Low	Mali Upper Volta	Somali Zambia		
High	Nigeria	Ghana Cameroon Congo (K)		

Only in the European case were higher levels of energy production, higher GNP, higher government expenditures, and more communications per capita correlated with the lower category of political violence. No such pattern displayed itself in the developing states.

Finally, an attempt was made to establish whether *increases* in economic standards and communications could be related to levels of violence —i.e., does development correlate with levels of violence? Again, there was no significant correlation. Per capita gross national product in nearly all cases grew from 1955 to 1965, whether the state was in the high or the low category of violence. Only four countries, three of which were high-violence cases, remained the same or declined. However, statistics were sufficiently unreliable in several countries to prohibit the formulation of firm conclusions. In total government expenditures per capita, only four states did not show increases—two high- and two low-violence cases. In communications—radios and telephones—and electricity production, every state but one showed growth. The material available did not allow us to draw conclusions on the basis of rate of growth. In sum, available data did not prove any correlation between increased income, output, production, and communications on one side and levels of violence on the other, although more reliable statistics might show variations based upon the rate of development.

Three obvious conclusions can be summarized here. First, our data did not support Mr. McNamara's contention that there was a constant relationship between economic level and violence. Obviously, there have been examples of violence generated by economic or social deprivation, but on the basis of our examination, these conditions cannot be flatly stated to be consistent causes of violence. Secondly, all should acknowledge that data reliability for the developing states was a constant problem which raises questions as to the utility of statistical analysis involving data from these regions.

Finally, this exercise suggests that analysis should be limited primarily to those states for which we have some confidence in the reliability of our information. In the meantime, every effort should be made to sort through data on developing areas, establishing points that are accurate, searching for new ways of gathering better data, and, most importantly, making clear to other researchers the reliability of the material employed. Under these conditions the development of aggregate data will provide better building blocks for future research.

SUMMARY AND CONCLUSIONS

7

The foregoing chapters have attempted to illustrate the extent to which political violence has varied in type of conflict, supporting rhetoric, and causation. Emphasis has been given to domestic political violence leading to death or injury, and no effort has been made to cover what some consider more subtle forms of violence such as imprisonment, slavery, preventive detention laws, thought control, and so forth. Nor have primarily international conflicts been investigated, although the postwar world has found it increasingly difficult to differentiate between civil and international issues. However, domestic violence in itself provides a wide enough area of study, for it has been the cause of deaths and injuries in the millions during the postwar decades. What then have we learned from this particular study of political violence?

TYPES Domestic political violence can be divided into primordial (religious, racial, and ethnic), revolutionary, coup, separatist, and specific issue-oriented (particularly student and electoral) forms of violence. Each of these forms of conflict brought death or injury in a substantial number of the 123 countries investigated. Three types were experienced in approximately 50 percent of the states (student and electoral in 53 percent, coup in 48 percent, and primordial in 43 percent), while the other two were found in a quarter of the sample (revolutionary in 29 percent and separatists in 22 percent).

Considerable variety existed both within and between regions. Thus, primordial and separatist violence was very low in Latin America (8 and 4 percent respectively), showing the general homogeneity of the area and the maturation of the nation-building process. At the same time, coup violence was slight in Europe (3 percent), displaying the greater stability of institutions there. Strangely enough, revolutionary conflict touched only 8 percent of the African states analyzed. Cross-regionally, the number of countries affected by all forms of violence was smallest in Europe, with Latin America a distant second. Thus, the newer Afro-Asian countries, with their myriad of basic problems attendant to forging new political institutions; have been the centers of domestic political conflict in the postwar years.

Other variations also were noted in our analysis of the forms of worldwide conflict. First, there appears to be a difference in the levels of casualties among the different types of violence. The highest number killed during the past generation has been from ideological and primordial tensions, as illustrated by the widespread conflicts of this type in Colombia, Pakistan, India, Vietnam, Cambodia, Rwanda, Sudan, China, and Burma. Certain classes of violence have produced relatively low casualty figures, particularly student and electoral disputes (with rare exceptions such as the elections in the Philippines and events in East Pakistan in 1971). Coups have tended to result in very low casualties at the immediate moment of overthrow, with deaths coming more often after the coup when rivals are being eliminated.

Secondly, it should be noted that political violence is rarely related to one issue or cause. Normally, it is part and parcel of a complex interrelationship of political, economic, and cultural forces. This complexity, plus the absence of reliable data in many cases, should warn the observer against simplistic classifications and analyses. The debates over issues and causes of conflicts in Indo-China, Hungary, the American ghettos, and East Pakistan are cases in point.

RHETORIC   An analysis of the rhetoric of political violence may lead either to moral repulsion or simply to cynicism. The justifications presented by the extreme right and left, as well as by the spokesmen for primordial groups and governments, often display superficial as well as fundamental similarities. We have seen five justifications for reactive violence which have gained some notoriety across ideological and cultural barriers.

1. Defense of the group or society has been and remains a traditional reason for the employment of violence. Today tribal and religious groups use it as justification for war against neighbors, the Ku Klux Klan uses it to defend white culture, the East Pakistanis to protect their lives and homes, and the state to control revolutionaries, critics, power rivals, and others.

2. Vengeance is an emotional issue providing focus to efforts to inflict

pain and suffering on those who have wronged the group. It has been the battle cry of Bengalis in East Pakistan, Africans in Zanzibar, blacks in America, anti-government forces in Hungary, and colonial peoples throughout Afro-Asia who have risen against real or purported past wrongs perpetrated by those believed to have been their oppressors.

3. Often the opposition has been described as immoral, amoral, incompetent, "undesirable," and/or generally a danger to present or longed for values. "Godless Communism," "immoral wars," "criminal types," "nihilists," "traitors," "Kafirs," and other labels too numerous to list have been used to portray the enemy or his position. Because the opponent does not maintain or support the proper values, it is a moral act to war against him.

4. Violence has been presented as a means of achieving unity within the group. Revolutionary organizations have discussed the cathartic effect of violence as a means of inspiring and welding together its members. Governments, seeking to develop internal support, have employed violence against groups or individuals unpopular with the people.

5. Finally, most perpetrators of violence within and without the government have noted the necessity of using force in particular circumstances. The justifications have been varied and normally are accompanied by protestations of long-range peaceful intentions. It is argued that violence was necessary because of the intransigence of the opposition and its unwillingness to compromise, or that force was deployed only after peaceful means of persuasion were unsuccessful.

Our analysis of the rhetoric of violence, however, should not induce us to forget that rhetoric is not necessarily correlated with acts of violence. Some individuals, groups, and even nations employ emotional rhetoric as a tactic or cultural trait without any intention of suiting action to words. If certain statements made by Chinese Communist leaders, Arab nationalists, and some young militants had been made by Western European governments, they would preface major conflict. It is, therefore, important that the reader analyze a piece of rhetoric within the political or cultural environment of the particular spokesman for violence.

CAUSES   The causes of political violence have been so numerous and complex that some scholars have argued that the very uniqueness of each conflict defies efforts to formulate cross-national hypotheses. One United States Government survey concluded:

There is no single cause . . . which is more or less potent. In fact usually there are multiple causes and important contributing conditions rooted in historical relationships and brought to violence by a variety of catalysts. . . . Each conflict has been unique.[1]

This does not mean that general hypotheses cannot be drawn from the wide variety of violent events that have transpired during the postwar years. Three possible causes for domestic political conflict have been analyzed here.

First, it is noteworthy that exceptionally high casualties have resulted from situations where a communal group has perceived that it is subjugated economically, politically, or socially by another primordially based class. The stresses wrought by this condition may develop into large-scale violence through a single catalytic event which disturbs traditional patterns of interaction. Such events were the elections in Malaysia, the overthrow of Prince Sihanouk in Cambodia, and the coming of independence in Rwanda and Zanzibar. Through the analysis of several case studies we have seen that this combination of politico-economic and cultural tensions can lead to extremely emotional conflicts with high casualties. In fact, in Cambodia, Rwanda, Nigeria, and Zanzibar substantial population groups felt sufficiently endangered to seek refuge in other countries. At the same time, these conditions may smolder for a lengthy period with low levels of violence, and it is remarkable that greater conflict has not ensued between primordial elements in places such as Malaysia, the United States, Canada, and Belgium.

A second and more complex element to be considered is that of legitimacy. To what extent have the institutions of a given society developed or maintained the loyalty of the people and provided the framework for non-violent interaction? Here we are analyzing more than governmental stability as it is normally understood by political scientists, for this question also entails the interrelationship of other societal foundations such as family and church. In our brief comparison of Burma and Thailand, it was noted that in the former the colonial impact weakened or destroyed more than the Burmese monarchy and independence: it also had a devastating effect on all levels of political authority, the religious community, the educational system, economic patterns, and public order. These changes can be loosely correlated with increased domestic disorder. In contradistinction, the more evolutionary development of the continuously independent Kingdom of Thailand produced loyalty to its social and political institutions, bringing with it stability and relative domestic tranquility.

Finally, the argument has often been presented that high levels of violence can be correlated with lower economic and social standards.

---

[1] *Wins II: A Worldwide Integral Strategy for 1970*, pp. 3–48, quoted in Brown, 1967, p. 3.

Among the propositions forwarded by American defenders of foreign aid is the statement that economic and social development is necessary in order that violence be diminished. Given the questionable nature of the data for the developing nations, it is extremely difficult to test this proposition using aggregate data. However, from the data we do have it appears that there is no significant correlation between economic and social standards and national levels of political violence. More research is demanded in this area prior to making firm conclusions.

These were but three of a multitude of possible causes for domestic political conflict. The fact that internal disorder has not abated, as illustrated by recent events in Cambodia, Northern Ireland, and East Pakistan, underlines the necessity for greater study of this phenomenon. The interrelationship of internal crises and international wars in Indo-China and the Indian subcontinent lends further urgency to our search for causes and solutions.

SELECTED BIBLIOGRAPHY

African Centre. n.d. *Rwanda: Land of a Thousand Hills.* Essex: Nore Press.

ALTBACH, P. G. 1970. "Student Movements in Historical Perspective," *Journal of Southeast Asian Studies,* I (March), 74–84.

ANDERSON, CHARLES, FRED R. VON DER MEHDEN, and CRAWFORD YOUNG. 1967. *Issues of Political Development.* Englewood Cliffs, N.J.: Prentice-Hall, Inc.

ANDRUS, J. RUSSELL. 1947. *Burmese Economic Life.* Stanford: Stanford University Press.

ANTUNES, GEORGE. 1971. "Socio-economic, Political, and Violence Variables as Predictors of Government Expenditures in Nations: 1955, 1960, 1965." Unpublished Ph.D. dissertation, Northwestern University.

BASS, J. 1970. "The PKI and the Attempted Coup," *Journal of Southeast Asian Studies,* I, No. 1 (March), 96–105.

BLACK, CYRIL, and THOMAS THORNTON, eds. 1965. *Communism and Revolution.* Princeton: Princeton University Press.

BOCCA, G. 1968. *The Secret Army.* Englewood Cliffs, N.J.: Prentice-Hall, Inc.

BOYD, ANDREW. 1969. *Holy War in Belfast.* Tralee, Ireland: Anvil Press.

BRACKMAN, ARNOLD. 1969. *The Communist Collapse in Indonesia.* New York: W. W. Norton & Company, Inc.

BREITMAN, GEORGE, ed. 1965. *Malcolm X Speaks.* New York: Grove Press.

BRODERICK, FRANCIS, and AUGUST MEIER, eds. 1965. *Negro Protest Thought in the Twentieth Century.* Indianapolis: Bobbs-Merrill Company.

BROWN, S. 1967. *Political Violence and Political Development.* Rand Document D–15327.

BRZEZINSKI, Z. K. 1956. *The Permanent Purge.* Cambridge: Harvard University Press.

Burma Round Table Conference. 1932. *Proceedings, 27th November 1931–12th January 1932.* London: HMSO.

Burmese Government. 1949. *Report of the Land and Agriculture Committee:* Part I: *Tenancy;* Part II: *Land Alienation.* Rangoon: Government Printing.

The Burning Question. n.d. Rangoon: Thein Press.

BWY, DOUGLAS. 1968. "Political Stability in Latin America: The Cross-Cultural Test of a Causal Model," *Latin American Research Review,* III (Spring), 17–66.

CADY, JOHN. 1958. *A History of Modern Burma*. Ithaca: Cornell University Press.

CHRISTIAN, JOHN. 1945. *Burma and the Japanese Invader*. Bombay: Thacker & Company, Ltd.

CLARK, RAMSEY. 1970. *Crime in America*. New York: Simon and Schuster, Inc.

COLEMAN, J. 1958. *Nigeria: Background to Nationalism*. Berkeley: University of California Press.

DAS KHOSLA, GOPAL. n.d. *Stern Reckoning*. New Delhi: Bhawanani & Sons, Publishers.

DEMARIS, O. 1970. *America the Violent*. New York: Cowles Education Corp.

DE PAAR, LIAM. 1970. *Divided Ulster*. Middlesex: Penguin Books, Ltd.

DEVLIN, BERNADETTE. 1969. *The Price of My Soul*. New York: Alfred A. Knopf, Inc.

DONNISON, F. S. V. 1970. *Burma*. New York: Frederick A. Praeger, Inc.

DRAPER, THEODORE. 1967. *Israel and World Politics*. New York: Viking Press.

ECKSTEIN, H., ed. 1963. *Internal War: Problems and Approaches*. New York: The Free Press.

ENDLEMAN, S., ed. 1968. *Violence in the Streets*. Chicago: Quadrangle Books.

ENLOE, CYNTHIA. 1967. "Multi-Ethnic Politics: The Case of Malaysia." Unpublished Ph.D. dissertation, University of California.

FURNIVALL, J. S. 1948. *Colonial Policy and Practice*. Cambridge: Cambridge University Press.

GAGLIANO, FELIX. 1970. *Communal Violence in Malaysia, 1969: The Political Aftermath*. Athens, Ohio: Ohio University Center for International Studies.

GEERTZ, CLIFFORD. 1960. *The Religion of Java*. New York: The Free Press.

GELTMAN, MAX. 1970. *The Confrontation*. Englewood Cliffs, N.J.: Prentice-Hall, Inc.

GILLESPIE, JOAN. 1960. *Algerian Rebellion and Revolution*. New York: Frederick A. Praeger, Inc.

GRAHAM, H., and TED GURR, eds. 1969. *The History of Violence in America*. New York: New York Times.

GURR, TED. 1968. "A Causal Model of Civil Strife: A Comparative Analysis Using New Indices," *American Political Science Review*, LXII (December), 1104–24.

————. 1970. *Why Men Rebel*. Princeton: Princeton University Press.

HANNA, WILLIAM. 1971. "Student Protest in Independent Black Africa," *Annals of the American Academy*, 395 (May).

HASTINGS, MAX. 1970. *Barricades in Belfast*. New York: Taplinger.

HERRICK, A., et al. 1968. *Area Handbook of Tanzania*. Washington, D.C.: American University.

HINDLEY, DONALD. 1964. *The Communist Party of Indonesia, 1951–1963*. Berkeley: University of California Press.

HO CHI MINH. 1960–62. *Selected Works*. Hanoi.

HUGHES, JOHN. 1967. *Indonesian Upheaval*. New York: David McKay Co., Inc.

HUNTINGTON, S. 1968. *Political Order in Changing Societies*. New Haven: Yale University Press.

INGRAM, JAMES. 1955. *Economic Change in Thailand since 1850*. Stanford: Stanford University Press.

Israelis Reply. 1970. No. 14 (January).

KIRKHAM, JAMES, SHELDON LEVY, and WILLIAM CROTTY, eds. 1970. *Assassination and Political Violence.* New York: Bantam Books

LEMARCHAND, RENÉ. 1970. *Rwanda and Burundi.* London: Pall Mall Press.

LOFCHIE, MICHAEL. 1965. *Zanzibar: Background to Revolution.* Princeton: Princeton University Press.

MCNAMARA, ROBERT S. "Security in the Contemporary World," *Department of State Bulletin,* LIV (June 6), 874–81.

MCNEIL, ELTON B. 1966. "Violence and Human Development," *Annals of the American Academy,* 364 (March).

MCVEY, RUTH. 1970. *The Social Roots of Indonesian Communism.* Brussels: Centre d'étude de sud-est asiatique et de l'extrême-orient.

MAQUET, JACQUES. 1961. *The Premise of Inequality in Rwanda.* London: Oxford University Press.

MATHEWS, HERBERT. 1970. *Fidel Castro.* New York: Simon and Schuster, Inc.

MAUNG HTIN AUNG. 1965. *The Stricken Peacock: Anglo-Burmese Relations, 1752–1948.* The Hague: Nijhoff.

——————. 1967. *A History of Burma.* New York: Columbia University Press.

MERAY, T. 1969. *That Day in Budapest.* New York: Funk & Wagnalls.

Middle East Record. 1961. Tel Aviv: University of Jerusalem.

NIEBURG, H. L. 1969. *Political Violence.* New York: St. Martin's Press.

NWANKWO, A., and S. IFEJIKA. 1969. *The Making of a Nation: Biafra.* London: Hurst.

O'BALLANCE, E. 1966. *Malaya: The Communist Insurgent War, 1948–60.* Hamden, Conn.: Archon Books.

Office of Strategic Services. 1944. *Japanese Domination of Thailand.* Washington, D.C.: Government Printing Office.

——————. 1944. *The Problem of Law and Order in Burma under British Administration.* Washington, D.C.: Government Printing Office.

PURCELL, VICTOR. 1957. *The Chinese in Modern Malaya.* Singapore: Donald Moore.

PYE, LUCIEN. 1956. *Guerrilla Communism in Malaya.* Princeton: Princeton University Press.

——————. 1962. *Politics, Personality, and Nation Building: Burma's Search for Identity.* New Haven: Yale University Press.

RABIBHADANA, AKIN. 1969. *The Organization of Thai Society in the Early Bangkok Period, 1782–1873.* Data Paper 74, Ithaca: Cornell University Press.

RATNAM, K. J. 1965. *Communalism and the Political Process in Malaya.* Kuala Lumpur: University of Malaya Press.

RIDDELL, P. 1970. *Fire over Ulster.* London: Hamish Hamilton.

ROWAN, CARL. 1967. *Los Angeles Times* (December 6).

SCHANCHE, DON. 1970. *The Panther Paradox.* New York: David McKay Co., Inc.

SCHWARZ, WALTER. 1968. *Nigeria.* London: Pall Mall Press.

SEGAL, AARON. 1964. *Massacre in Rwanda.* Fabian Research Series, No. 40. London: Fabian Society.

SILCOCK, T. H., and E. FISH, eds. 1963. *The Political Economy of Independent Malay.* Berkeley: University of California Press.

SILVERSTEIN, J. 1970. "Burmese and Malaysian Student Politics: A Preliminary Comparative Inquiry," *Journal of Southeast Asian Studies*, I (March), 3–22.

SIRISUMPUNDH, KASEM. 1962. "Emergence of the Modern National State in Burma and Thailand." Unpublished Ph.D. dissertation, University of Wisconsin.

SKLAR, R., and C. WHITAKER. 1966. "The Federal Republic of Nigeria," in G. Carter, ed., *Regionalism in Eight African States*. Ithaca: Cornell University Press.

STEINBERG, DAVID, et al. 1957. *Cambodia: Its People, Its Society, Its Culture*. New Haven Human Relations Areas Files.

————. 1971. *In Search of Southeast Asia*. New York: Frederick A. Praeger, Inc.

United States Agency for International Development. 1967. *Proposed Foreign Aid Program FY 1968*. Washington, D.C.: Government Printing Office.

VELLA, W. 1955. *The Impact of the West on Government in Thailand*. Berkeley: University of California Publications in Political Science, Vol. 4.

VITTACHI, TARZIE. 1967. *The Fall of Sukarno*. New York: Frederick A. Praeger, Inc.

"Voices of Revolution." 1966. *The Harvard Review*, IV.

VON DER MEHDEN, FRED R. 1963. *Religion and Nationalism in Southeast Asia*. Madison: University of Wisconsin Press.

————. 1960. "Burma's Religious Campaign against Communism," *Pacific Affairs*, XXXIII (September), 290–99.

————. forthcoming. "The Secularization of Theravada Buddhism in Burma and Thailand," in Donald Smith, ed., *Religion and Politics in Asia*. New Haven: Yale University Press.

WALKER, DANIEL. 1968. *Rights in Conflict*. New York: Bantam Books.

WALKER, RICHARD. 1955. *China Under Communism: The First Five Years*. New Haven: Yale University Press.

WALLACE, M. 1970. *Drums and Guns: Revolution in Ulster*. London: Geoffrey Chapman.

WERTHEIM, W. 1966. "Indonesia before and after the Untung Coup," *Pacific Affairs*, XXXIX (Spring–Summer), 115–27.

WILLIAMS, MASLYN. 1970. *The Land In Between*. New York: William Morrow & Co., Inc.

WILLMOTT, WILLIAM. 1967. *The Chinese in Cambodia*. Vancouver: University of British Columbia Press.

WILSON, DAVID. 1962. *Politics in Thailand*. Ithaca: Cornell University Press.

WOLFGANG, MARVIN E., ed. 1966. "Patterns of Violence," *Annals of the American Academy*, 364 (March).

ZADROZNY, MITCHELL, ed. 1955. *Cambodia*. Chicago: University of Chicago Press.

ZIMMERMAN, CARLE. 1931. *Siam: Rural Economic Survey, 1930–31*. Bangkok: Bangkok Times Press.

INDEX